**The Fundamental
Beliefs for
Preschoolers**

Love Letters from Jesus

ROSANNE C. TETZ

REVIEW AND HERALD® PUBLISHING ASSOCIATION

Since 1861 | www.reviewandherald.com

Devotional

Credits

This book was
Edited by Cheryl Woolsey
Copyedited by Jocelyn Fay and James Cavil
Designed by Patricia S. Wegh
Illustrations by Mary Bausman
Typeset: 11/13 New Century Schoolbook

PRINTED IN U.S.A.

12 11 10 09 08   6 5 4 3

R&H Cataloging Service
Tetz, RosAnne C., 1953-
    Jesus loves me, too.

    1. Children—Religious life.   2. Devotional
literature—Juvenile.   3. Devotional calendars—
Seventh-day Adventist.   I. Title.

242.62

ISBN 978-0-8280-1516-5

To order additional copies of
Love Letters From Jesus, by
RosAnne C. Tetz, call **1-800-765-6955.**
Visit our website at **www.rhpa.org**
for information on other
Review and Herald products.

Dedication

To Drew and Cassie.
Believe.

My Little Devotional

Contents

Contents

Contents

Contents

Contents

Contents

Contents

Contents

Contents

Contents

Contents

Contents

Contents

Contents

Dear Mom and Dad...

Is it possible for preschoolers to understand what it means to be a Seventh-day Adventist? Yes, the gospel is simple enough for a child to understand, yet deep and wide enough for scholars to study forever.

These devotionals are designed to introduce the fundamental beliefs of Seventh-day Adventists to young children. Each day's lesson will engage your children by involving them in activities that both illustrate the point and give them something to do. They are fun.

But more important, these lessons will give your children a broad, firm foundation of biblical truths. Now, when they are soaking up so much information each minute; now, when they are young and eager to learn; now they can know what the Bible teaches about what God is like.

These lessons follow God's plan for our world from Creation to the new earth. They are more or less in chronological order. It would probably be best if you could use them in order, because some concepts build on others. But it's not critical—go ahead and skip around. A few of the devotionals on the same topic will involve making a book or other handiwork in which a portion is completed each day. These lessons should be done in order.

Present the devotionals in the style that works best for you. It helps a lot if you can read them ahead of time and gather the materials you will be using.

Most of the lessons use materials to involve your children in learning. You probably have most of the items already—things such as crayons, paper, and glue. Use substitutions if you need to, and feel free to adapt the lessons to fit your child's situation.

Some of the devotionals will involve writing words or reading from the Bible. This isn't meant to imply that your preschool children should read. It's just a good idea for young children to see words being written and used.

The Bible version used throughout is the *International Children's Bible.* This translation was prepared specifically for children.

We hope that you and your children will enjoy learning about the doctrines of our church. Our prayer is that these devotionals will help you and your child know God, understand His plans, and choose to follow Him.

Look In!

Materials: *a smudged and dirty mirror; a Bible; window cleaner; newspaper*

"God's word is alive and working." Hebrews 4:12.

S*how the dirty mirror.]* Look at this mirror! Can you see all the smudges? What happens when you press your hands against the mirror? It gets even more smeared. When we look **at** this mirror we see that it is a dirty mirror.

Now let's look **in** the mirror. We won't look at the smudges this time, we'll look at the face in the mirror. Who do you see? Is your face clean? Is your hair combed? That's what a mirror is for—so we can see how we look. A mirror is to look in.

[Show a Bible.] You know what this is! It's a Bible! There are different ways to see the Bible.

We can look **at** the Bible and see just a book. (Just as we looked **at** the mirror and saw only the smudges.)

Or we can look **in** the Bible and learn about God and how He loves us and helps us! (Just as we looked **in** the mirror and saw what we looked like.) The Bible is for us, right now. The Bible is to look in.

I want to look **in** the Bible and learn more about God, don't you? And I want to clean up this dirty mirror! Will you help? *[Child sprays mirror with cleaner and wipes it with crumpled newspaper.]*

Dear Jesus, thank You for the Bible. Amen.

#1

Theme: The Bible

Message From God

Materials: *a letter or e-mail message; a storybook; a parenting or women's magazine*

"It really is God's message."
1 Thessalonians 2:13.

D o you know what this is? It's a letter. *[The person who wrote it]* couldn't come and talk to us, so he/she sent this message instead. It would be wonderful to see *[this person]* and talk together face-to-face, but we can't. It's a good thing we can send letters.

In the Garden of Eden, God talked to Adam and Eve face-to-face. After they disobeyed, sin separated them from God. They couldn't talk to Him face-to-face anymore. But God wanted to tell people that He loved them. He wanted them to know He had a plan to save the world from sin.

So God had people write about it. That's how the Bible was written.

The people who wrote the Bible did not write stuff they made up themselves. God told them what to write. Sometimes God sent these writers a dream. Sometimes He gave them ideas. They wrote down His messages.

The Bible is a special book. *[Show storybook.]* This book tells stories. So does the Bible. But they aren't the same. *[Show magazine.]* This magazine gives advice. So does the Bible. But the Bible is more than stories and advice. The Bible is full of words God has spoken. That's why we call it the Word of God.

Dear God, help me listen to Your words. Amen.

Theme: The Bible

#2

Taste and See!

Materials: *a small dish holding a little honey, covered by a larger bowl; a spoon*

"Your promises are so sweet to me. They are like honey to my mouth!" Psalm 119:103.

There's a surprise under this bowl. Can you guess what it might be? Here is a hint: It tastes sweet. Close your eyes and open your mouth and I will put a little of it on your tongue. *[Give them a taste of the honey.]* Do you know what it is?

Honey is very sweet, isn't it? Sometimes when we like something we say it is "sweet." We might even call someone we love "honey"!

We can't see God. Just like we couldn't see the honey that was hiding under this bowl. But we can learn about God from the Bible. The Bible tells stories of the things God has done. The Bible gives us God's messages. The Bible shows us what God is like.

David wrote a song about learning to know God. His song says, "O taste and see that the Lord is good" (Psalm 34:8, KJV). What does he mean? How can you taste that? You can listen to the words in the Bible! Then you will see that God is good. Then you will learn about God.

What do you think David's song sounded like? Can you make up a tune?

Dear God, I want to learn about You. Amen.

#3

Theme: The Bible

A Lamp for My Feet

Materials: *a blanket; a flashlight; a long piece of yarn or string*

"Send me your light and truth. They will guide me." Psalm 43:3.

L et's play a game. We'll pretend it's a dark night and we want to walk through the forest. *[Make the room as dark as possible.]* This piece of yarn will be the path we want to follow. We'll put this blanket over our heads to make it seem darker.

How will we see in the dark? You hold the flashlight. Shine it down at the floor so we can see the yarn. The light will help us follow the path out of the forest. *[Use the flashlight to help you see to walk along the yarn path.]*

It's fun to play with a flashlight. A flashlight is useful, too. When it is night a flashlight helps us see. A flashlight can help us find our way.

The Bible is like a flashlight. A Bible writer wrote a song that says, "Your word is like a lamp for my feet and a light for my way" (Psalm 119:105).

The Bible can show you the way. When things seem dark and confusing, the Bible can help you see the right thing to do. You can think about the stories of Jesus and other people in the Bible. The Bible is like a light. It can help you make the right choices.

Dear Jesus, I want to follow Your light. Amen.

Theme: The Bible

#4

It's the Truth

Materials: *a picture book with an animal who wears clothes and speaks; Bible storybook with pictures. Adapt the following [bear, Jericho] to fit your books.*

"Your teaching is truth." John 17:17.

L et's look at the pictures in this book. There's something funny here. Look, this [bear] is wearing clothes. Do bears really wear clothes? No. And these bears are talking to each other. Do bears know how to talk like humans? No. This story is just pretend. It didn't really happen.

Sometimes we tell stories with animals doing people things, like talking or playing games. We know animals can't really do those things. The stories are a way for us to talk about how people behave. In this story the little bear learns [it is important to obey]. When we read it, we can see that [it is important for little people to obey], too.

Some stories are just pretend. Some stories are true. It's important to know the difference.

Let's look at the pictures in this Bible book. In this story God's people shout and the walls of Jericho fall down. Can people make a big stone wall fall down by shouting? No. But God can. The wall fell because the people obeyed and because God helped them. This story shows us that God can do anything. It shows us that it is important to obey God.

This is a true story. It really happened. The stories in the Bible are true. They are not pretend.

Dear Jesus, thank You for the true stories in the Bible. Amen.

#5

Theme: The Bible

Be Wise

Materials: *various things to ask questions about, such as toys, picture of animals, paper and pencil, crayons, fruit, clothing*

"The Scriptures are able to make you wise." 2 Timothy 3:15.

L et's play a game. I'll show you something and you tell me what it is. *[Adapt your questions to the things your child knows (e.g., show a ball; show a picture of an animal; write an alphabet letter on a piece of paper; ask what color something is; hold up some fingers and ask how many).]*

You are learning so many things! Every day you learn more. I am so proud of you.

Let's play again. This time I will ask you to make a choice. *[Examples: show a box of crayons and ask which is their favorite; show several kinds of fruit and let them choose their favorite; get out some of their T-shirts and ask*

which is their favorite.]

You are able to make choices! You know what you like. I hope you will always make good choices.

The Bible helps us learn. No matter how smart we get or how many things we know, there is always more to learn in the Bible. The Bible helps us make good choices. It helps us know the right thing to do.

When someone is always learning and making good choices, we say they are wise. The Bible can make you wise.

Dear Jesus, help me to be wise. Amen.

Theme: The Bible
LLFJ-4

#6

Count on It

Materials: *something to drop, such as a pillow; something to jump off, such as the couch*

"Every word of God can be trusted."
Proverbs 30:5.

There are some things that always happen. Every morning the sun comes up. Why don't you pretend you are the sun coming up? Crouch down in a little ball. Now it's morning! Rise into the sky!

There are some things you can always count on. Every spring the flowers grow. Can you pretend to be a flower? First you are just a little seed, then you grow and grow and grow. Hold your leaves and your petals up to the sunshine.

There are some things you can be sure of. Take this pillow and drop it. What happened? It fell to the floor. What will happen if you try it again? It will fall. It will always fall. You can count on it.

There are some things you can trust. Would you like me to catch you? Climb up on the couch. Tell me when you are ready. Then jump. I will catch you. You can trust me.

You can trust God. He is always there. He is always the same. He will always do what He says.

You can trust the Bible. It is the Word of God. He always keeps His word. He always tells the truth.

Dear God, I trust in You. Amen.

#7

Theme: The Bible

Read the Instructions

Materials: *a game that comes with instructions, for example, a board game such as Candyland*

"I have taken your words to heart so I would not sin against you." Psalm 119:11.

D o you want to play this game? OK, let me see if I can remember how to play. You try to put the game pieces on your head and then you sing a song. No? H'mmm. Oh, I know. You tilt the board like this and slide the pieces down. *[Make up a few more silly ways to play.]*

I can't guess any more ways to play this game. How can I find out the right way to play? Oh, look! Here are some instructions. If we read them, we will know how to play this game.

The people that made this game sent these instructions so we will know how to play. The way to have the most fun is to follow these instructions.

The Bible has instructions. God wants us to be happy. The Bible tells us how we can be happy. The Bible has instructions on how to live a good life. These instructions help us know the right thing to do.

The Bible tells us how God loves us and saves us from sin. If you want to be God's child, the Bible will tell you everything you need to know.

Dear Jesus, help me to follow Your instructions. Amen.

Theme: The Bible

#8

Tell Me a Story

Activity: *charades*

"Lord, tell me your ways. Show me how to live." Psalm 25:4.

Let's play a game called charades. I'll act out a story, and you try to guess which story it is. *[Act out a Bible story that is well known to your child (e.g., Zacchaeus).]*

Would you like to have a turn? Can you think of a story to act out for me? *[Help your child act out a Bible story for you to guess.]*

I like that game. It's fun to act out stories, and it's fun to guess what they are.

People like to hear stories. We like to read stories together. We like to tell each other stories. We like to hear about other people and the things that happen to them. We like stories.

Stories are a very good way for us to learn.

When someone in a story makes a bad choice, we can learn from their mistake. When someone in a story learns a lesson, we can learn it too.

God knows how wonderful stories can be. That's why the Bible is full of really good stories. God loves to tell us stories. That's one way we can learn more about Him. That's one way we can learn how He wants us to live.

Dear Jesus, thank You for telling us stories. Amen.

#9

Theme: The Bible

Praise Him, Praise Him

Materials: *a piece of paper and crayons, or old magazines, scissors, and glue*

"Sing to the Lord and praise his name." Psalm 96:2.

Close your eyes and think about your favorite food. Without making any sounds at all, imagine taking a big bite. Remember, you can't say a word!

Now, take another imaginary bite, but this time you can say "Mmmmmm" or "That's yummy" or anything you want.

Which bite tasted better? Which was more fun? When we can say we like something, it helps us like it even more.

That's why we praise things. When we praise something, we say how good and important and valuable it is. We tell other people. When we see something beautiful, like a rainbow

or a butterfly, we say, "Oh, look!"

The Bible is full of praise. There are many poems in the Bible that tell God how great He is for making this wonderful world. There are many songs that sing praise to God for His love and care.

Listen to this song: **"Sing** to the **Lord** and **praise** His **name**."** *[Say it with exaggerated emphasis on the bold words. Also, clap on those words to create a rhythm. Keep repeating it, and encourage your child to join in.]*

Let's make a book of praise. *[Fold a piece of paper in half to create a four-page book. Draw pictures of things for which you give praise.]*

Dear God, I sing praise to You. Amen.

Theme: The Bible

#10

Devotion

Letters for You

Materials: *a letter or other piece of mail; crayons and paper*

"Using the Scriptures, the person who serves God will be ready." 2 Timothy 3:17.

Look what we got in the mail! *[Talk about the letter, whom it's from, etc.]* It's fun to get mail. Did you know there are letters in the Bible? Several of the books in the Bible are actually letters that were written a long time ago. Many of the letters were written by a man named Paul.

Paul traveled around teaching about Jesus. In each place, some people would believe in Jesus, and they would start a church.

Then Paul would go preach in another city. But he missed the people in the churches he left behind. So he wrote them letters. *[For an example, look at Ephesians 1:1, to see who the letter is from and to.]*

In his letters he gave advice, he helped solve problems, he taught about God. When we read these letters in the Bible we learn about God.

Paul didn't actually write the letters. He had a friend, called a scribe, who helped. Paul would walk around the room and talk, while the scribe wrote down his words as fast as he could. Then Paul would sign his name.

Would you like to be a scribe? When you hear me say a color, you pick that crayon up and make a mark on this paper. If I say "Green," pick up the green crayon and make a green mark.

Dear Jesus, thank You for the letters from our friend Paul. Amen.

#11

Theme: The Bible

The Word of God

Materials: *Prepare for this story by "painting" the outline of a heart on a piece of paper, using lemon juice or vinegar and a little paintbrush. Let it dry. You will also need the stove burner or some other heat source.*

"My love will never disappear."
Isaiah 54:10.

When we say, "The Bible is the Word of God," we mean that the Bible has messages from God. It sounds strange to say "The Word." That makes it sound like there is just one word in the Bible. You can see that the Bible has lots and lots of words. When we say "The Word of God" we mean all the things He tells us.

But if we were going to choose just one word to be the Word of God, do you know what that word would be? Let's pretend it's a secret message and we are going to discover it. *[Take the paper you have prepared; carefully hold it about six to eight inches from the burner. The heat will bring out the heart shape.]*

Can you see the heart? When you see a heart shape, what word do you think of? Sometimes we use it as a symbol for love.

If the Word of God was just one word, that word would be "love." Over and over in the Bible, God tells us "I love you." All the stories, and all the poems, and all the letters, tell us: "God loves you." That is the message He wants us to remember always.

Would you like to paint a secret message? *[Let everyone make a secret lemon juice picture.]*

Dear God, thank You for loving me. I love you. Amen.

Theme: The Bible

#12

There Is Only One God

Materials: *clay*

"The Lord is our God. He is the only Lord." Deuteronomy 6:4.

Let's play with clay. I think I'll make a snowman. What will you make?

Do you like my snowman? He was fun to make. But he's just a toy. He can't do anything. Can my snowman dance? No. I can pretend. I can pick him up and wiggle him. *[Demonstrate.]* But he's not really dancing—I'm making him dance.

When the Bible was being written, there were some people who didn't believe in God, a real God who made them. They wanted a god they could see, so they made idols.

They made many different gods out of clay or wood. They pretended that these idols brought rain or made the crops grow. But these gods were not real. They couldn't really bring rain or make the crops grow. People made them up. The idols were not real, just as my snowman is not real.

The real God does not want us to make that mistake. He tells us we should not worship idols. He tells us that He is the only God.

There is only one God—the God who created us.

Dear God, I will worship only You. Amen.

Theme: The Trinity

Three Names

Materials: *paper and pencil*

"The grace of the Lord Jesus Christ, the love of God, and the fellowship of the Holy Spirit be with you all."
2 Corinthians 13:14.

Y ou have three names: a first name, a middle name, and a last name. Do you know what your three names are? I'll write them down to show you what they look like. *[Write your child's names on three separate lines.]*

One, Two, Three. You have three names. But how many people are you? You are just one person—one person with three names.

God also has three names. His three names are: God the Father, God the Son, and God the Holy Spirit. God is three persons with three names.

God is three persons, but He is only one God—one God with three names.

Do you have a nickname? Sometimes, instead of calling you by all your names, do we call you another name for short? Do any of your friends have nicknames?

My name is *[first] [middle] [last].* But you call me *[Mommy/Daddy].* That is one of my names that I like best.

God has other names too. Sometimes we call God the Father "Jehovah." Sometimes we call God the Son "Jesus" or "Jesus Christ." Sometimes we call God the Holy Spirit the "Holy Ghost." They are all names for the same wonderful God.

Dear God, I will praise Your name. Amen.

Theme: The Trinity

#14

One and Three at the Same Time

Materials: *three lengths of heavy cord 18 inches or longer; different kinds of rope, clothesline, twine, yarn, string, etc.*

"There is one God and Father of everything. He rules everything. He is everywhere and in everything." **Ephesians 4:6.**

Knot the cords and tie or nail the cords down on one end so your hands are free to demonstrate braiding.] Can you count how many cords we have? Yes, we have three cords. I'm going to braid them together so we have one rope. *[Demonstrate, and allow your child to practice as long as this activity is fun.]* Now we have one strong rope! We started with three cords, but when they are braided together, they make one rope.

Let's look together at how these other pieces of rope and string are made. *[Unravel the ends of each rope, and discuss how some are twisted, some are wrapped, etc.]*

God is three persons, and one God. Just as our rope has three separate cords, God is three persons. But all together, our cords are one rope, just like our God is one God.

God the Father, God the Son, and God the Holy Spirit are all different, and they do different things. But they work together as one God. They each love us and want to help us, and they help each other take care of us.

Dear God, I want to learn more and more about You. Amen.

#15

Theme: The Trinity

God Works Together

Materials: *cotton balls, two dolls [representing your child and Jesus], paper heart*

"Let us, then, feel free to come before God's throne." Hebrews 4:16.

God the Father, God the Son, and God the Holy Spirit work together. Let me show you one way: they work together when you pray. Let's pretend this doll is you. You want to pray. How does God help?

When you pray, you talk to the Father in heaven. Let's fluff these cotton balls and pretend they are clouds. We'll put the clouds up high [e.g., on a shelf] and pretend that is heaven.

When we pray, God the Son takes our prayers to the Father. Let's pretend this doll is God the Son. We'll put it next to your doll to show that He is helping you pray.

The Holy Spirit is the one who helps you want to pray in the first place. Sometimes we say God's Spirit is inside us. Let's put this little paper heart on your doll to show that the Holy Spirit helps you want to pray.

God the Father is the Person to whom you are praying *[point to cotton clouds]*. God the Son is the Person who takes your prayers to God *[point to the dolls]*. And God the Holy Spirit is the Person who helps you want to pray *[point to the heart]*. They all work together when you pray.

Dear God, thank You for helping me pray. Amen.

Theme: The Trinity

God Loves You

Activity: *a walk outside*

"God is love." 1 John 4:16.

Go on a walk. Search for a tree that has one trunk and three main branches.]

Look at this tree. How many branches does this tree have? How many trees are there? It has three branches, but it is only one tree. Each of these branches is different, but they all belong to the same tree.

This tree makes me think of God. There is only one God, but God has three persons—God the Father, God the Son, and God the Holy Spirit.

Let's pretend this is a fruit tree. What kind of fruit do you wish was growing on it? *[Let child choose.]* I wish *[a different fruit]* was growing on

this tree. Let's pretend that one branch could grow *[child's choice],* one branch could grow *[your choice]* and one branch could grow *[a third kind of fruit].*

Do trees really grow that way? No. An apple tree grows only apples. An orange tree grows only oranges. A tree is the same in all its branches.

So is God. The Father, Son, and Holy Spirit are three different persons, but They think alike.

This is what God thinks: "I love you." God the Father loves you. God the Son loves you. God the Holy Spirit loves you. God loves you.

Dear God, thank You for loving me. Amen.

#17

Theme: The Trinity

A Holy Name

Activity: *play with words*

"Let everyone praise his holy name forever." Psalm 145:21.

L et's play with the word "think." First let's play catch. I'll say "think" then you say "think," and we'll toss it back and forth to each other. *[Play word catch for a minute.]*

Now let's play copycat. If I say "think" in a high voice, then you say it with a high voice. *[Try it low, fast, slow, singing, three times fast, etc.]*

Now let's just say "think" together, over and over, for 30 seconds.

If you use a word over and over, after a while it loses its meaning. By the end of this game, "think" was only a noise to me. It didn't mean anything; it was just a sound I could make.

There are some words that are very important. We must never let them become just a noise. Their meaning is too precious. Sometimes we say these words are holy.

God the Father's name is Jehovah. Jehovah is a holy name. We don't say it very much because we don't want it to lose any of its meaning.

We don't say it often because we don't want to be disrespectful. Angels cover their faces when they say God's name. We must be careful too. God's name is holy.

Dear God, I want to honor Your holy name. Amen.

Theme: God the Father

Devotion

#18

God Is Good

Materials: *a photo of your child, something that smells good, something that feels good (such as fur, a cat, or a stuffed animal), something that tastes good*

"Thank the Lord because he is good. His love continues forever." Psalm 118:1.

You look good in this picture. I like the way you are smiling. I like *[your hat, your eyes, etc.].* You look good.

Close your eyes and smell this *[perfume].* Doesn't it smell good? When I smell this it makes me think about *[flowers, summer, rain, etc.]* What does it make you think about? This smells good.

One of my favorite sounds is when you laugh. What sounds good to you? *[the phone, singing, a cat's purr, etc.]*

Now close your eyes and feel this. Doesn't it feel good? What do you think it is? What does it feel like? When I feel this I want to fill my fingers full of it and rub it on my cheek. This feels good.

Now for a real treat. It looks good and it smells good, but best of all, it tastes good. Would you like some? Doesn't it taste good?

We say these things are good because they are just what they should be. They make us happy. This *[strawberry]* tastes like it should. When you laugh, the sound makes me happy.

Do you wonder what God is like? Most of all, God is good. God is perfectly what He should be. He is just right. He is good in every way.

Dear God, I thank You because You are good. Amen.

Theme: God the Father

We Can't See God Now

Materials: *doll or action figure, pillows, flashlight*

"Teach me what I cannot see." Job 34:32.

Do you wonder what God looks like? That's a hard question because no one can see God the Father. God is too holy. He is too good. His holiness and goodness are so bright that if people saw Him they would die.

Some people have seen God in a dream, but that is not the same as seeing Him in person. The closest someone has come to seeing God the Father would be Moses. That's an interesting story.

Moses and God were good friends. Moses wanted to see God. When he asked God if he could see Him, God said, "You cannot see my face. No one can see me and stay alive" (Exodus 33:20).

But God found a way for Moses to see Him. He put Moses in a large crack in a rock. He covered Moses with His hand. Then God took away His hand and let Moses see His back.

Even with all that protection, God's goodness was so bright it made Moses' face shine. Moses saw God's goodness. He remembered it all his life.

Let's act out this story. This doll will be Moses. You can hide him here in these pillows and cover him with your hand and shine the flashlight on him. You do the actions while I read the story. *[Read Exodus 33:20-23.]*

Dear God, I want to know You. Amen.

Theme: God the Father

#20

All About God

Materials: *paper, crayons, stapler*

"Know that the Lord is God. He made us, and we belong to him." Psalm 100:3.

Let's make a book about you. I'll write "My name is" and then you write your name. On this page I'll write "I am a *[boy/girl]*." Then you draw a picture of yourself. What color are your eyes? [Check in the mirror.] I'll write "My eyes are [brown]." You draw a picture of your eyes with a [brown] crayon.

[As long as it is fun, continue making pages on hair, favorite color, favorite food, pets, family, house, etc. Staple it into a book.] This is a wonderful book. It tells all about you.

The Bible is a book that tells us about God. *[Staple six papers together to make another book. On each page, write the following bolded words*

from Exodus 34:6.]

The Bible says God told Moses, **"I am the Lord."** Sometimes the Bible writers did not want to write "Jehovah" because it is such a holy name. So they wrote "the Lord" instead.

God told Moses, "The Lord is a God who **shows mercy** and is **kind**." God said, "The Lord **doesn't become angry quickly**." God told Moses "The Lord has great **love** and **faithfulness**." These words tell about God.

God wants us to know what He is like. He tells us in the Bible.

Dear God, thank You for telling us all about You. Amen.

#21

Theme: God the Father

God So Loved the World

Materials: *pencil and paper. As you tell the story, each time you come to a choice, quickly sketch the two options, then circle the one that your child chooses.*

"For God loved the world so much that he gave his only Son." John 3:16.

I'm going to tell a story, and you can help me make some choices. Should this story be about a boy or a girl? What will his/her name be?

[Name] likes to watch his mother cook. Sometimes he helps pour and stir. When they cook on the stove, [Name]'s mom always says, "Don't touch the burner." But [Name] thinks the red burner is pretty, and one day he puts his finger on the burner. It really hurts. What should his mom do? Should she spank him or put his hand in cold water and try to make it feel better?

[Name]'s mom decides to take him to the doctor. The doctor wraps his sore finger in a bandage. Then it's time to pay the bill. Should his mom make [name] pay the doctor, or should she pay? The nurse gives [name] a treat. Should it be a lollipop or a sticker?

[Name] burned his finger because he disobeyed. But his mom took care of him. She helped him feel better, and she paid his doctor bill.

This story reminds me of what God did for us. When we disobey God, we should be punished. We really should die for what we've done. But God loved us so much He sent His Son to take our punishment. Jesus paid for what we did.

Dear God, thank You for taking my punishment. Amen.

Theme: God the Father

#22

Jesus Is God and Man

Materials: *something your child really likes—e.g., a certain game or book, a toy (a new surprise or an old favorite), a snack, an activity (trip to the playground)*

"The Word became a man and lived among us." John 1:14.

I'm thinking of something you like. Can you guess what it is? *[Give hints and encourage your child to ask questions to discover it.]* You figured it out! Now, tell me all the things you like about this treat/ activity. *[Elicit as much discussion as you can.]*

It's fun to play guessing games about things we like, and it's nice to talk about things we like, but the best thing of all is to actually **do** the things we like.

God wanted people to know how much He loved them. He sent messages so people could **hear words** about what He was like. People could **talk about** God's love. But God thought that if they could actually see Him and hear Him and touch Him, then they could understand.

So God the Father and God the Son made a plan. They decided that God the Son would come to earth to live with people. He would hide His brightness and holiness inside a human body so people could look at Him. His name would be Jesus. People could learn about God by knowing Jesus.

And that's what happened. Jesus came to earth. He was both God and man. People could see Him and hear Him. He taught us about God.

Now, let's quit guessing and talking. Let's *[have treat / do activity].*

Dear God, thank You for sending Jesus. Amen.

#23

Theme: God the Son

Jesus Came to Teach

Activity: *act out the parable*

"Jesus used many stories to teach them." Mark 4:2.

One of Jesus' favorite ways to teach us about God was by telling stories. Once Jesus told a story about a farmer planting seeds. *[Read Mark 4:3-8 together. Talk about how to act out each verse (e.g., how to scatter seed, peck like a bird, pretend to be a sprout, etc.). Then read the passage aloud while your child acts it out.]* Jesus says this story can show us how people learn about God. Some things in the story are symbols—they stand for other things. The seed is a symbol for God's teaching. The different kinds of soil are the different kinds of people who hear about God.

Remember when the birds ate the seed? That ground is too hard. The seed can't grow in the hard ground, so the birds find it. The hard ground is a symbol for people who don't want to learn about God.

Remember when the sprouts wither in the sun? That stands for people who won't let God's teaching go deep into their lives. They give up. The plants that were choked by weeds are symbols for people who don't take time to learn about God. But some seeds fall in good soil and grow into fine plants. They are the people who obey and tell others about what He has said.

Dear Jesus, thank You for telling us stories. Amen.

Theme: God the Son

#24

Jesus Came to Heal

Materials: *a blindfold, some coins, picture of Jesus*

"He followed Jesus, thanking God."
Luke 18:43.

Here is a story about one way Jesus showed God's love. Let's act it out. Your name will be Bartimaeus. Bartimaeus is blind. *[Blindfold or close eyes.]*

One day Bartimaeus's friend led him from his house to a spot by the side of the road where he could sit and beg for money. *[Lead child.]* Bartimaeus sat down and called, "Help the blind!" *[Child calls.]* Every once in a while someone put a coin in his hand. *[Give coins.]*

Then Bartimaeus heard lots of people talking and coming his way. Bartimaeus asked, "What's going on? What's happening?" Finally someone told him, "Jesus is coming here."

Bartimaeus had heard that Jesus could help blind people see. This was his chance to see. He started to shout, "Jesus, please help me!" The people around him told him to be quiet, but Bartimaeus wouldn't be quiet. He shouted more and more.

Jesus stopped and said, "What do you want?" Bartimaeus said, "I want to see again." Jesus said, "OK," and Bartimaeus could see. What do you think was the first thing he saw? Jesus! *[Hold up picture of Jesus, then take off blindfold.]*

Bartimaeus learned about God's love. Jesus helped him see.

Dear Jesus, thank You for showing us God's love. Amen.

#25

Theme: God the Son

Jesus Sends a Helper

Materials: *bubble bath or dish soap; a bathtub, sink, or dishpan; water*

"When I go away I will send the Helper to you." John 16:7.

Make bubbles; play with them until they disappear.] *Where did all the bubbles go? They disappeared into the water. The bubbles were lots of fun when we could see them and play with them, but we can't see them anymore.

Jesus was here on earth for a while. People could see Him and hear Him and touch Him. But then He was killed. Jesus took the punishment for our sins.

Jesus did not stay dead. He came back to life. He told His followers that He was going to go back to heaven to be with God the Father. His friends were worried. They didn't want Jesus to go away.

Jesus told them not to be worried. He told them not to be afraid. He promised that someday He would come back to get them. And He promised that He would always be with them.

How could Jesus be with them if He was in heaven? Jesus said He would send a Helper to take His place. Who is this Helper? It is God the Holy Spirit.

Jesus went back to heaven, but the Holy Spirit is here with us now. People could see Jesus, but we can't see the Holy Spirit. Just like we can't see these bubbles anymore. They are invisible.

Dear Jesus, I want to know more about the Holy Spirit. Amen.

Theme: God the Holy Spirit

#26

The Holy Spirit Is Everywhere

Materials: *a globe*

"He will give you this Helper to be with your forever." John 14:16.

I've noticed that you know how to breathe really well. Let's practice breathing right now. Breathe in. Breathe out. You're very good.

I wonder if you can breathe in another room. Let's go into another room and practice breathing in and out. Obviously you breathe the air in the house very well. Let's go outside and get some fresh air. Breathe in and out. Very good.

I wonder if you would breathe this well in another country. Look at this globe. It is a picture of our world. We live here. Let's find a country on the other side of the world. Do you think you could breathe in *[China]?* I'm sure you could. You can breathe anywhere there is air, and there is air all around our world. There is air for everyone to breathe.

God the Father and God the Son sent God the Holy Spirit to always be with us. You may wonder how the Holy Spirit can be with you and be with a person in China at the same time. He can. The Holy Spirit can be anywhere.

God sent the Spirit to be your Helper and my Helper; He helps our neighbors, and the people in all the countries all over the world.

The Holy Spirit can be everywhere, just like air.

Dear God, thank You for sending the Holy Spirit to be with me. Amen.

#27

Theme: God the Holy Spirit

The Spirit Is Contagious

Activity: *yawning*

"He will tell about me. And you also must tell people about me." John 15:26, 27.

Let's pretend that you are sleepy. Show me how you can yawn and stretch. You're a good yawner.

Do you know why people yawn? They need more air. Show me again what happens when you yawn. See how your mouth opens wide? You are getting a big gulp of air.

Just now you yawned on purpose, but usually a yawn happens without your thinking about it. When you get sleepy, your brain thinks that if only it could have more air you could stay awake. So your brain tells you to yawn. Sometimes that wakes you up a little.

One of the funniest things about yawns is that they are contagious. When I see you yawn, it makes me want to yawn too. Sometimes just talking about yawning makes me want to yawn! Oh no, I think I'm going to yawn now!

God sent the Holy Spirit to help us know that God loves us and to help us want to learn about God. How does the Holy Spirit do that?

The Holy Spirit does this by helping us see things and wonder about ideas. And, like a yawn, these ideas are contagious. The Holy Spirit shows us about God's love, and we want to know more. The Holy Spirit helps us learn about God.

Dear God, I want the Holy Spirit to help me learn about You. Amen.

Theme: God the Holy Spirit

#28

The Spirit Gives Us Gifts

Materials: *stand-ins for items used in church (i.e., offering plate, hymnal, pulpit)*

"There are different kinds of gifts; but they are all from the same Spirit."
1 Corinthians 12:4.

Let's think about the different things that happen in church. *[Let your child think of activities that take place at church. Ask your child to demonstrate what each activity is like. For instance, if your child says, "We sing," have him/her show you what it is like and perhaps sing a song. Props (such as a pulpit) can help in the demonstrations.]*

Lots of different things happen at church. People sing and preach and play the piano and pray and take up the offering. We need people to do all these things. How do people know how to do all these different things?

The person who plays the piano/organ proba-bly took music lessons and practiced for years. The person who preaches probably went to school to learn how to preach and spends many hours preparing the sermon.

These people have a Helper who helps them do these things. Do you know who that Helper is? The Holy Spirit. The Bible says the Holy Spirit gives us gifts. Some people have the gift of preaching. Some people have the gift of singing. Because we have these gifts we are able to help others.

You are able to show me the things that happen at church because you have been watch-ing. The Holy Spirit has given you gifts too.

Dear Jesus, thank You for these gifts. Amen.

Theme: God the Holy Spirit

The Spirit Gives Us Power

Activity: *memory and exercise games*

"The Holy Spirit will come to you. Then you will receive power." Acts 1:8.

It's important to eat a good breakfast. The *[toast]* you ate this morning gives you the energy you need to run and play. Food gives you power.

Let me see some of that power now. Let me see you jump with both feet. Can you jump 10 times? *[Jump and count.]* Excellent!

Do you know why you can jump? You have strong muscles. The more you use your muscles, the stronger they get. Your muscles give you power.

Now I'm going to ask you some questions. *[Tailor the questions to your child's level of knowledge—e.g., Count to 10. Say the alphabet. How old are you? What color is the couch?]* You know so many things! Do you know why? You are using your brain power.

Food gives you power. Your muscles give you power. Your brain gives you power. Do you know what else gives you power? The Holy Spirit.

Before Jesus went back to heaven, the last thing He said was, "The Holy Spirit will come to you. Then you will receive power."

What kind of power does the Holy Spirit give? He gives power to do the right thing. Power to know the truth. Power to tell others about Jesus. The Holy Spirit gives us power.

Dear God, thank You for giving me power. Amen.

Theme: God the Holy Spirit

LLFJ-7

#30

From A to Z

Materials: *the alphabet, written out in order*

"I am the Alpha and the Omega, the Beginning and the End." Revelation 21:6.

Do you know what this is? It's the alphabet. Let's sing the song about the alphabet. *[Point to the letters as you sing.]* That was great. *[If this activity was boring for your child, try it again—backward.]*

We can use all these letters to make words. And we can use words to tell about our ideas.

What is the name of the first letter of the alphabet? *[Point.]* A. What is the name of the last letter? *[Point.]* Z.

In the last book of the Bible, God says that He is like the alphabet.

God is like the letter A because He is the beginning of all things. He created everything. Everything comes from God.

God is like the letter Z because God is the end of all things. God is the goal. God is what makes everything complete.

God is like the whole alphabet, from A to Z. Everything that is alive begins and ends in God.

[Point to the A and slowly sweep through the alphabet as you say:] We were created by God. God takes care of us. He saves us from sin. And someday God will take us to heaven and we will be with Him again.

Dear God, help me find my beginning and end in You. Amen.

#31

Theme: The Trinity

He Is
Your God

Materials: *Bible [mark texts with sticky notes to find them quickly]; paper, photo or crayons*

"I will be your God." Jeremiah 30:22.

The Holy Spirit helps us learn about God. Jesus came to earth so we could see how much God loves us. And God gives us the Bible so we can read about Him. Let's look in the Bible to find out more about God. The Bible shows us that God belongs to everyone. *[Turn to Jeremiah 32:27 and read, "I am the God of every person on the earth."]*

But sometimes the Bible says that God belongs to a certain group of people. *[Turn to 1 Chronicles 16:36 and read, "Praise the Lord, the God of Israel, forever and forever."]* And sometimes the Bible says that God belongs to a certain person. *[Turn to Psalm 46:11 and read,*

"The God of Jacob is our protection."]

And the Bible says that God belongs to you. *[Turn to Jeremiah 30:22 and read, "So you will be my people, and I will be your God."]*

God is the God of the universe. He is the God of Abraham, Isaac, and Jacob. And God is the God of *[child's name]*. You are God's child, and He is your God.

[At the top of the paper write, "I belong to God." Your child can draw a picture or glue a photo of himself or herself on the page and decorate it.]

Dear God, I am happy we belong to each other. Amen.

Theme: The Trinity

#32

Perfect Peace

Materials: *This is a hold-on-your-lap-and-snuggle kind of story.*

"We pray that the Lord of peace will give you peace at all times and in every way." 2 Thessalonians 3:16.

Would you like to know one of my favorite secret things to do? I like to come peek at you when you are sleeping! When you are fast asleep in your bed you look like a little angel. Everything is quiet and peaceful. I think about all the fun we have been having. I feel happy and peaceful. Do you ever get a feeling like that?

Before our world was created there was peace in heaven. The angels were all happy and peaceful. They saw that God's rules were fair and would make them happy. The angels could choose if they wanted to serve God, and they did. God loved the angels and they loved Him.

There was peace in heaven because the angels chose to follow God's rules. No one got in trouble. Everyone got along. Everyone was happy.

Some people think peace means "no war." But it's more than that. In the Bible, peace means having everything you need to be happy.

I like to look at you when you are sleeping because you are peaceful. I feel peaceful right now, sitting here with you and holding you. I love you.

Dear God, thank You for Your perfect peace. Amen.

Theme: The Great Controversy

Lucifer

Materials: *paints or crayons, paper, a black marker*

**"People who are proud will be ruined."
Proverbs 18:12.**

Would you like to make some pictures? *[Let your child draw anything, while you draw an angel. When you are finished, admire the pictures.]*

How would you feel if someone with a black marker scribbled all over your lovely picture? I guess you'd be surprised and upset and sad.

In God's perfect heaven, before our world was made, Lucifer was the leader of the angels. He was beautiful and smart. All the other angels thought he was wonderful. He was free to do anything he wanted. But Lucifer started thinking about how wonderful he was. He became proud of how smart and beautiful and important he

was. He didn't want to remember that God had made him that way. *[Scribble a little on your angel picture with a black marker.]*

Then Lucifer became jealous. It bothered him that God had more honor than he did. *[Scribble some more.]* Lucifer became selfish. He wanted all the power and glory. He didn't want anyone else to have any. *[More scribbles.]*

When Lucifer began to sin, it was as if he were scribbling all over a perfect picture. Sin messes up the beautiful, perfect, peaceful life God has given us.

Dear Jesus, please put Your perfect peace in my heart. Amen.

Theme: The Great Controversy

#34

War in Heaven

Materials: *a bunch of small toys (such as blocks), or clothespins, pennies, or something similar to manipulate while you tell the story.*

"He and his angels lost their place in heaven." Revelation 12:8.

Let's tell a story with these *[toys].* First we'll put them into rows of three. One, two, three . . . *[Try to line up about 10 rows before anyone gets bored.]*

Now let's pretend these *[toys]* are angels in heaven. Lucifer, the leader of the angels, has been causing trouble. *[Hold one of the toys up to represent Lucifer.]* He has become proud and selfish. Now he wants to start a rebellion—he wants the other angels to follow him instead of God.

Lucifer complains to the angels that God is not fair. He says they shouldn't have to follow God's rules. The angels are confused. They admire and love Lucifer. They know how smart he is. What is going on?

Some angels listen to Lucifer. They decide they don't want to follow God's rules anymore either. Other angels are very upset. They beg Lucifer to ask for forgiveness. God is patient. He pleads with Lucifer to stop making trouble. But Lucifer won't listen.

God calls a meeting. He says that only those who follow the laws of heaven can stay. One third of the angels decide to leave with Lucifer. *[Remove one "angel" from every row.]* Now there is peace in heaven again, but it feels empty.

Dear God, I want to follow Your rules. Amen.

#35

Theme: The Great Controversy

In the Beginning

Materials: *paper bag, opened out with top folded closed; flashlight; blanket; picture or photo*

"Then God said, 'Let there be light!'"
Genesis 1:3.

I'll open this bag, and you peek inside. Now I'm going to guess what you saw in there. Was it big? Was it red? Did it wiggle? H'mmm. I give up. What's in there? Nothing! This bag is empty!

In the beginning our world was empty. There was nothing here—no people, no animals, no plants. It was empty. It was dark. There was nothing.

Then God decided to create our world. He started at the beginning.

Would you like to see the first thing God made? Look in the bag. What do you see? Nothing. It's dark and empty. Now, watch this.

Then God said, "Let there be light!" *[Shine flashlight into bag.]* What's in the bag now? Light! God made light. God saw that the light was good.

Light is good. We need light to see. Let's go under this blanket where it's very dark. I'm putting something in the bag now. *[Put picture in bag.]* Peek inside. Can you see it? No. It's too dark. Now, shine the flashlight in the bag. Can you see anything? The picture was there before, but we needed the light to see it. We need light to see.

Dear God, thank You for creating light. Amen.

Theme: Creation

#36

God Made Light and Shadows

Materials: *flashlight; paper or cardboard; scissors, popsicle sticks, glue*

"He divided the light from the darkness." Genesis 1:4.

When God made light, He also made shadows. Light cannot shine through some things. Light cannot shine though your hand. Look at this. *[Make the room as dark as possible. Tell child to hold up his/her hand in front of a wall. Shine a flashlight on the hand.]* This light comes from the flashlight. When the light hits your hand, it stops. It can't shine through your hand. So the other side of your hand is dark. We call that darkness a shadow.

Shadows can be fun to play with. We can learn how to hold our hands in a certain way and make shadow pictures. You hold the flashlight and I am going to try to make a shadow picture with my hands. Now I'll hold the flashlight while you make a shadow picture. If you move your hands you can make the picture move.

You can have a shadow puppet show. *[Choose a familiar story, such as Daniel and the Lion's Den. Cut out simple shapes of Daniel, the king, a lion, an angel. Glue them on popsicle sticks. As you tell the story, let your child manipulate the puppets so that the shadows illustrate the story.]*

Dear God, thank You for creating shadows. Amen.

Theme: Creation

God Made Colors

Materials: *paper, crayons; garden hose; soap bubbles*

"I am putting my rainbow in the clouds." Genesis 9:13.

When God made light, He hid a surprise inside. I am going to give you some hints. See if you can guess. *[Draw a rainbow with the crayons. Use the colors in this order: red, orange, yellow, green, blue, purple.]* It's a rainbow. This rainbow is made with crayons, but a real rainbow is made out of light.

Regular light has all the colors of the rainbow blended together. Sometimes the light is broken open, and all the colors come dancing out.

What can break the light? Raindrops. Sometimes we can see a rainbow if the sun comes out from behind the clouds just as the rain is stopping. The sun shines through the raindrops, the raindrops bend the light, and all the colors shine out.

We don't see rainbows in the sky every day. They are a special treat. But we can try to make a rainbow. *[If it is a sunny day, stand with your back to the sun and make a fine spray with the hose—sometimes a rainbow will shimmer in the water drops. Or blow some soap bubbles and look for the rainbows wiggling inside.]*

God didn't make everything the same color. He gives us all the colors of the rainbow.

Dear God, thank You for creating colors. Amen.

Theme: Creation

God Made Air

Materials: *blue fingerpaint, a big piece of paper, newspaper to cover the table*

"God made the air to divide the water in two." Genesis 1:7.

On the first day of creation, God made light. The next day, God created air. This is how the Bible describes it: "God made the air to divide the water in two. Some of the water was above the air, and some of the water was below it" (Genesis 1:7).

Let's make a picture of this. First let's make the water below the air. The waters below the air are the oceans, rivers, and lakes. *[Put some blue fingerpaint on the bottom part of the paper. Show your child how to slide his/her fingers up and down in the paint to make waves.]*

Now let's make the water above the air. What do you think the water above the air could be? It's clouds! The clouds are made of little drops of water. When it rains, the raindrops fall from the clouds. Let's add clouds and raindrops to our painting. *[Show child how to swirl the paint to make clouds. Make raindrops with fingertips.]*

God put the air between the oceans and the clouds. We don't live in the ocean, and we don't live in the clouds. We can't live in the water. We need air to breathe. That's why God made air.

Dear God, thank You for creating air. Amen.

#39

Theme: Creation

We Can't See the Air

Materials: *two balloons*

"The wind blows where it wants to go."
John 3:8.

On the second day of Creation God made air. Air is all around us. I'm going to blow some air out of my mouth. Watch. Could you see the air? No. We can't see air, but it's there.

Now, watch this. I'm going to blow some air into one of these balloons. *[Blow up one balloon. Compare the empty balloon to the full balloon.]* Can you tell which balloon is full of air? We can't see the air, but we can see what it does. The air fills up this balloon.

We can't see the air, but we can feel it sometimes. Can you feel this? *[Hold the balloon by the child's arm and let a little air out.]* We can feel the air when it moves. You can make the air move by fanning yourself. *[Demonstrate.]* You can feel the wind when it blows.

We can't see the wind blow. But if we could see it, this might be what it looks like. *[Fill the balloon with air again, then release it so that it flies around the room. Let your child retrieve it; blow it up again, and let him / her release it.]*

Even though we can't see it, air is important.

Dear God, I'm glad You made the air and the wind. Amen.

Theme: Creation

#40

We Need Air and Water

Activity: *pantomime*

**"The rivers of God are full of water."
Psalm 65:9.**

On the second day God made air. It's a good thing He did. We need air to breathe. All day and all night, we breathe air. We breathe in. *[Take an exaggerated breath in and hold it a moment.]* We breathe out. *[Exaggerated breath out.]* In and out, in and out. *[Have child breathe slowly with you.]*

Animals breathe air too. Show me how a dog breathes. That's right. In and out. Show me how a bird breathes. In and out. Show me how a fish breathes. Wait! A fish lives in the water. It doesn't breathe the same way we do. A fish breathes the air in the water. Even plants need air to breathe.

God put the air between the water below and the water above. It's a good thing He made water. We need water too—for a million reasons. I am going to pretend to do something with water. You guess what I'm doing. *[Pantomime different activities involving water, e.g., drinking, washing hands, brushing teeth, flushing toilet, bathing, swimming, watering plants. You can take turns.]*

People need water. Animals need water. Plants need water. God knows how important water is. On the second day of creation God made air and water.

Dear God, thank You for air and water. Amen.

#41

Theme: Creation

God Made Land

Materials: *a big bowl or tub; a washcloth or hand towel; water*

"You built the earth on its foundations."
Psalm 104:5.

On the first day of Creation God made light. On the second day He made air. On the third day God made land.

David wrote a poem about when God made land. Listen:

"The mountains rose.

The valleys sank.

The water went to the places you made for it." (Psalm 104:8)

Before God made the land, the world was covered with water. *[Fill a big bowl about half full of water.]*

God told the water to gather together into oceans, and the dry land appeared. *[Put a wet washcloth or hand towel into the bowl of water. You may need to add more water.]*

The mountains rose. The valleys sank. *[Let your child help you pull sections of the towel up to form mountains and valleys.]*

Now there was land. People need land. If we didn't have land, we'd have to live on boats. Animals need land. If animals didn't have land, they'd have to swim all the time, like fish. Plants need land. If plants didn't have land, they wouldn't have a place to grow.

God knew we'd need it. So on the third day of Creation God made land.

Dear God, thank You for creating land. Amen.

Theme: Creation

#42

God Made Plants

Materials: *fruits, vegetables, a piece of wooden furniture*

"Then God said, 'Let the earth produce plants.'" Genesis 1:11.

On the third day of Creation God made land. He saw that the land was good, but He decided to make it even better. He decided to decorate it. So God said, "Let the earth produce plants." And then the land was covered with grass and bushes, flowers and trees. Now, that was good.

Plants are very beautiful. When you go to a park and see all the green leaves and grass, it just makes you feel good. And there's more than green. There are flowers in all the colors of the rainbow. And there's more than colors. There are delicious smells. Flowers smell wonderful. But so do trees. And don't you love the smell of grass when it's being mowed? Plants are lovely. But they are also helpful. People need plants.

What is this? *[Show fruits and vegetables.]* These are plants. Plants are very good for us to eat.

What is this? *[Show furniture.]* It is made of wood. Wood comes from trees. People use plants to build houses and make furniture.

When God made plants on the third day, He created many beautiful, useful gifts for us.

[Take a walk to look at plants. Talk about the names of the plants and how they help us.]

Dear God, thank You for creating plants. Amen.

#43

Theme: Creation

God Made Seeds

Materials: *tomato, apple, peanut*

"I have given you all the trees whose fruits have seeds in them. They will be food for you." Genesis 1:29.

On the third day of Creation God made land and plants. He also thought of a way to make more plants. He decided that the plants would make seeds. He said, "Every seed will produce more of its own kind of plant."

Plants make seeds. A tomato plant makes tomato seeds. *[Cut open a tomato and look at the seeds.]* An apple tree makes apple seeds. *[Cut open an apple and look at the seeds.]* Each plant makes seeds that will grow into the same kind of plant. If we planted this apple seed, what kind of plant would grow?

Inside each seed is a baby plant waiting to grow. Look at this peanut. It is a seed that we like to eat. If we take it apart carefully, we can see the baby plant inside. *[Shell the peanut, then split the seed in half along the natural break. Look at the tip to see the tiny plant.]* This is the baby plant, and the rest of the seed is food for the baby plant when it starts to grow.

[This demonstration works even better with a dry lima bean that you've soaked in water overnight.]

When God made plants, He also made seeds. *Dear God, thank You for making seeds. Amen.*

Theme: Creation

#44

God Made Food

Materials: *something sweet, something salty, something sour*

"He gives food to every living creature. His love continues forever." Psalm 136:25.

We are glad God made air. We need air to breathe. But breathing is sort of boring. In and out, in and out. We don't pay much attention to it.

On the third day, when God made food, He decided that food would not be boring. God made lots and lots of different wonderful things for us to eat.

Food is important. We need to eat so we can grow and be strong. Food gives us energy. And food is interesting. There are so many different things to eat, and none of them taste the same.

Food can taste sweet. Close your eyes and open your mouth. I am going to give you some- thing sweet to taste. See if you can guess what it is. *[Place something sweet in your child's mouth, e.g., fruit, ice cream. Let them guess. Talk about other things that are sweet.]*

Now close your eyes again. I'll give you something salty to taste *[e.g., popcorn, pretzel].* Can you guess what it is?

Close your eyes one more time. Now I will give you a little taste of something sour *[e.g., lemon, pickle].* What do you think it is?

Food is fun. Aren't you glad that when God made food, He made it so interesting?

Dear God, thank You, thank You, thank You for making food. Amen.

Theme: Creation

God Made the Sun

Materials: *a penny, a lamp*

"The Lord's name should be praised from where the sun rises to where it sets." Psalm 113:3.

On the fourth day of Creation God made the sun.

The sun is very, very big. It doesn't look that big, does it? That's because the sun is very, very far away. When things get farther away, they look smaller. *[Demonstrate by showing a penny from far away and asking if it is heads or tails. Walk closer until your child can see it.]*

The sun is very big and very far away and very, very hot. The sun is so hot, we can feel the heat even though it is so far away.

We see the sun only during the daytime. But the sun is always there. Pretend this lamp is the sun. God made our world so that it spins around. Every day our world turns one turn. *[Pick up your child and face away from the lamp.]* In the morning the world turns us toward the sun. *[Turn toward the lamp.]* All day we can see the sun in the sky. The world keeps on turning. *[Turn away from the lamp.]* At night it gets dark because we are turning away from the sun.

The sun keeps us warm. It makes things grow. It gives us light. Aren't you glad God made the sun?

Dear God, thank You for making the sun. Amen.

Theme: Creation

LLFJ-9

#46

God Made the Moon

Materials: *a ball, a flashlight, paper and pencil*

"He made the sun and the moon. His love continues forever." Psalm 136:7.

The Bible says that God "made the brighter light to rule the day. He made the smaller light to rule the night" (Genesis 1:16). "The brighter light" is the sun. What do you suppose "the smaller light to rule the night" could be?

It's the moon! On the fourth day God made the sun and the moon.

The moon is shaped like a ball. *[Show ball.]* But sometimes we see different shapes. Sometimes the moon looks like a circle. Sometimes it looks like a half circle. Sometimes it is just a little sliver. *[Draw pictures to illustrate.]* How does it do that?

The moon doesn't have any light of its own. The light we see shining on the moon comes from the sun. *[Shine flashlight on ball.]* The sun shines on half of the moon at a time. So half of the moon has daytime and the other half has nighttime.

When the moon looks like a complete circle, we are seeing all of the daytime half. But the moon does not stay still—it spins. Because it turns, we can't always see the daytime half of the moon. Every night we see a bigger or smaller part of the moon.

God made a very interesting moon.

Dear God, thank You for creating the moon. Amen.

#47

Theme: Creation

God Made the Stars

Materials: *flashlight, paper, pencil*

"Praise him, sun and moon. Praise him, all you shining stars." Psalm 148:3.

On the fourth day of Creation God made the sun and moon. But He wasn't finished yet. He also made the stars.

Stars are very hot, like the sun. They are very big, like the sun. But they are even farther away than the sun, so they look even smaller. Stars are very, very, very far away.

The stars are always in the sky, even in the daytime. But we can't see them during the day because the sun is so bright. *[Make the room as bright as possible. Shine a flashlight on the wall.]* Can you see the light from the flashlight? There's too much other light. *[Make the room as dark as possible.]* It's easier to see the flashlight now. The flashlight was shining all the time, but when it got darker we could see it better. It's the same with the stars.

Do you like to look at stars at night? It might look like the stars are just scattered around, but they have special places in the sky. Some groups of stars look like dot-to-dot pictures. *[Poke holes in paper in the shape of the big dipper and shine a flashlight through it.]*

We like to look at stars. When we see them we think about how big and great God is.

Dear God, thank You for creating stars. Amen.

Theme: Creation

#48

God Made Birds

Activity: *bird-watching, feeding the birds*

**"I know every bird on the mountains."
Psalm 50:11.**

God made air and water, land and plants, sun and moon. Now, finally, on the fifth day, everything was ready for God to make some animals. God said, "Let birds fly in the air above the earth" (Genesis 1:20).

Birds are special. They have something that no other animal has. Can you guess what that is?

Do you think it might be wings? Birds have wings. But so do butterflies.

Birds can fly. Do you think flying is what makes birds special? Flying is very special indeed, but birds aren't the only ones who can fly. Bats can fly, and bats are not birds.

Birds can lay eggs. Could eggs be the answer? No. Crocodiles lay eggs, and crocodiles are not birds.

What do birds have that no other animal has? Feathers! Birds have feathers. Butterflies don't have feathers. Bats don't have feathers. Crocodiles definitely don't have feathers. Only birds have feathers.

Sometimes we call birds our "fine feathered friends." When God made birds, he made some special friends for us. *[Do some bird-watching; count how many birds you can see in five minutes. Feed the birds; put out bird seed.]*

Dear God, thank You for creating birds. Amen.

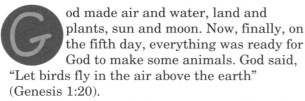

#49

Theme: Creation

God Made Fish

Materials: *paper cut in the shape of a fishbowl and fish; crayons; plastic wrap*

"Let the water be filled with living things." Genesis 1:20.

On the fifth day God created birds. That's not all. He also said, "Let the water be filled with living things." On the fifth day God created fish.

What do you breathe? You breathe air. What do birds breathe? Birds breathe air. Fish live in the water. Can you guess what fish breathe? Fish breathe air.

How can fish breathe air when they live in the water? Water has air in it! When God created fish, He gave them something called gills to help them breathe the air that's in the water.

If you watch a fish, you will notice that it opens and closes its mouth. *[Teach your child to* open and close his / her mouth like a fish.] Do you know why a fish does that? It's breathing! Water goes into its mouth and flows over its gills. The gills take air from the water.

People don't have gills, so we can't breathe the air that's in the water. When we go swimming, we have to put our heads out of the water to breathe.

Fish make nice pets. They are quiet and fun to watch. Let's make a paper fish pet. *[Glue fish to bowl. Draw some plants. Cover with plastic wrap to depict glass.]*

Dear God, thank You for creating fish. Amen.

Theme: Creation

#50

God Made Shells

Materials: *white glue, paintbrush, paper or cardboard, salt shaker, real shells or pasta shells*

"Look at the sea, so big and wide. Its creatures large and small cannot be counted." Psalm 104:25.

When God filled the water with living things on the fifth day of Creation, He made more than fish. Fish aren't the only things in the sea. There are octopuses and eels, shrimps and lobster. There are whales that look like big fish, but they aren't really fish. There are starfish that have "fish" in their name, but they aren't really fish either. Many, many interesting creatures live in the water.

It isn't easy to watch these creatures, because they live in the water and we don't. Can you think of ways that people can watch and learn about sea creatures? [*Snorkeling, scuba diving, submarines, aquariums.*]

We can look at shells. Shells are the homes for shellfish.

You have bones inside you. Can you feel the bones in your leg? Bones help you stand up and move around. If you didn't have bones, you would be like a puddle.

Shellfish don't have bones inside their bodies. They are little blobs. They need shells to protect them. Their shells are their houses.

[*Make a sandy shell picture. Thin glue with a little water. Brush it over the paper. Sprinkle salt on the glue. Glue shells onto the salted paper.*]

Dear God, thank You for making shells. Amen.

Theme: Creation

God Made Pets

Materials: *a list of ways pet owners take care of their pets; bowl of water, bowl of dry cereal, blanket, etc.*

"Let there be tame animals." Genesis 1:24.

G od filled the air with birds. He filled the water with sea creatures. Now, on the sixth day, God created animals that live on the land. God said, "Let the earth be filled with animals" (Genesis 1:24).

God said, "Let there be tame animals." Tame animals like to be around people. Pets are tame animals.

Pets depend on their owners to take care of them. Let's pretend you are my pet. I have a list here of things I need to do to take care of you. *[Check each item off your list when it's been acted out.]*

First, I need to give you water. *[Set a bowl on the floor. Let your child try to drink from it.]*

Next, I need to give you food. *[Put dry cereal in a bowl on the floor.]* Was that good?

Now you need a nice place to sleep. *[Fold up a blanket; your child pretends to sleep on it.]*

[Continue as you wish with exercise, bathe, brush, go to vet, play, etc.]

There's one thing left on my list. It says my pet needs lots of love. Climb onto my lap little pet, so I can hug you. God gave us pets to be our special friends.

Dear God, thank You for creating pets. Amen.

Theme: Creation

God Made Farm Animals

Activity: *make farm animal noises*

"Let them rule over the tame animals."
Genesis 1:26.

Pets are tame animals. Farm animals are tame also. God made farm animals on the sixth day of Creation. Some animals help people. The animals that live on the farm do many things for us. Let's play a game. I'll think of a farm animal, then I'll give you hints. You guess who I'm thinking of.

This animal has a tail. Its babies are called calves. This animal helps us by giving us milk. That's right; it's a cow. What sound does a cow make?

Here's another animal. It has feathers. Its babies are called chicks. This animal helps us by giving us eggs. It's a chicken. What sound

does a chicken make?

Ready for another one? This animal has four legs. Its babies are called lambs. It helps us by giving us wool. It's a sheep. What sound does a sheep make?

I'm thinking of an animal that is strong. Its babies are called foals. It helps us by giving us rides and pulling heavy things. It's a horse. What sound does a horse make? What sound does a duck make? What sound does a pig make? What sound does a rooster make?

God made farm animals to help us.

Dear God, thank You for creating farm animals. Amen.

#53

Theme: Creation

God Made Wild Animals

Materials: *On separate pieces of paper, draw: camel, polar bear, squirrel, tiger, mountain goat, raccoon, giraffe, rabbit.*

"Praise him, you wild animals."
Psalm 148:10.

On the sixth day God said, "Let the earth be filled with animals." God didn't make only tame animals. He made wild animals too.

Some animals do not need people to take care of them. They find their own food. They have their own homes in the forest or jungle or meadow. Here are some pictures of wild animals. Let's see if you can figure out where each of them lives.

Which of these animals lives in the desert? This animal can go for a long time without food or water. It can store extra food in the hump on its back. It's a camel. *[Let child help you color the background a "sand" color. Draw a palm tree.]*

Which of these animals lives in the ice and snow? This animal needs a fur coat to stay warm. It is the same color as snow so it can hide easily. It's a polar bear. *[Add an iceberg.]*

Which of these animals might live in a park or in your backyard? This animal is good at climbing trees. It likes to gather nuts and bury them. It's a squirrel. *[Color in some grass. Draw a tree.]*

[Continue as interest permits for tiger/jungle; mountain goat/mountains; raccoon/forest; giraffe/grasslands; rabbit/meadow.]

Dear God, thank You for making wild animals. Amen.

Theme: Creation
LLFJ-10

#54

God Made Reptiles

Materials: *paper and pencil; something made of leather, such as a glove; two pillows*

"God made the wild animals, the tame animals and all the small crawling animals." Genesis 1:25.

On the sixth day of Creation "God made the wild animals, the tame animals and all the small crawling animals." What are small crawling animals?

How about snakes? Most snakes are small. And snakes crawl. Snakes don't have any legs, so they can't walk. When they want to go someplace they slither. Can you slither like a snake?

Snakes are reptiles. A reptile is an animal that has scales. If you look at a snake's skin, you can see that it's made of little circles overlapping each other. *[Draw scales on paper.]* Some people think a snake's skin is slimy, but it isn't. It feels dry and cool, like this. *[Let child feel leather.]*

There are other reptiles. Lizards are reptiles. They have short little legs. Can you crawl like a lizard? Some lizards have pads on their feet that help them climb up walls. Can you climb walls? No, you can't.

Alligators and crocodiles are reptiles. They look like really big lizards.

Turtles are reptiles. They have shells. They can hide inside their shells and be safe from enemies. Pretend these pillows are your shell. Can you hide like a turtle?

God made reptiles on the sixth day.

Dear God, thank You for making reptiles. Amen.

#55

Theme: Creation

God Made Amphibians

Activity: *making an origami hopping frog or hopping like a frog*

"You must change your lives and do what is right." Jeremiah 7:5.

On the sixth day God made all the small crawling animals. Reptiles are small crawling animals. So are amphibians.

"Amphibians" It is fun to say. Amphibians. In another language, "amphibian" means "two lives." An amphibian is an animal that has two lives—well, not really. It has only one life. But that life is divided into two very different parts. In the first part of its life an amphibian is a water animal. In the second part it is a land animal.

Frogs are amphibians. They start their lives in the water. Frogs lay their eggs on top of the water. When the eggs hatch, out come little tadpoles. Tadpoles look like fish, with their big heads and long tails. Tadpoles breathe the air in the water, like fish. But they aren't fish. They're amphibians.

After a while the tadpole begins to turn into a frog. The tadpole begins to grow legs. The tail gets shorter and the legs get longer. Inside, the tadpole begins to grow lungs so it can breathe regular air. When the tail is gone and the legs are strong, the frog leaves the water and lives on the land.

[Make an origami hopping frog, or hop around like a frog.]

Dear God, thank You for making amphibians. Amen.

Theme: Creation

#56

God Made Insects

Materials: *three sections of an egg carton; six pieces of pipe cleaner*

"Go watch the ants." Proverbs 6:6.

Reptiles and amphibians are small crawling animals, but I can think of some animals that are even smaller and crawlier. Insects! Some insects are very small. Others are bigger, but not really big compared to other animals. (That's a good thing.)

Insects are crawly. Some can fly, but they all can crawl. They have six legs—all the better for crawling with.

Probably the most amazing thing about insects is that there are so many of them. They're everywhere! They are inside the house and outside. They are in the desert and in the jungle. Millions and millions of insects. Fortunately, insects are a favorite snack for lots of animals: birds, snakes, frogs, spiders. Otherwise, insects might take over the world.

Insects can be harmful. They get in our food and ruin it. They spread germs. Some insects bite and sting. But some insects are helpful. Bees might sting, but they also make honey. And they help fruit and flowers grow by spreading pollen around.

Insects can be fun to watch. Ants are very interesting. They are always busy, gathering food and working in their nest. *[Make an ant with an egg carton body and pipe cleaner legs.]*

Dear God, thank You for making insects. Amen.

Theme: Creation

God Made Spiders

Materials: *paper and pencil; black construction paper, scissors, stapler*

"You might get trapped by what you say. You might be caught by your own words." Proverbs 6:2.

God made small crawling animals on the sixth day of Creation. I'm thinking of another small crawling animal. Here are some hints: It lays eggs. It has eight legs. It spins webs to catch insects to eat. It's a spider!

How does a spider make a web? There are little tubes in the back of a spider. Something like thread comes out of these tubes. A spider attaches the thread at the top *[put pencil at top of page]* and drops down *[draw a line to the bottom]*. The spider spins more threads like this. *[Draw several "spokes."]*

Then the spider starts in the middle and spins bigger and bigger circles. *[Draw spirals around the spokes.]* When the web is finished, the spider sits in the middle and waits for flies to get caught in the sticky web. Dinner is served!

Why don't spiders get stuck in their own webs? The spiral is sticky, but the "spokes" are made out of thread that's not sticky. The spiders stay on the unsticky part.

[Make a spider hat. Cut a strip long enough to go around your child's head. Cut eight strips for the legs. Staple the "legs" around the headband. Draw eyes on a circle; staple it to the front.]

Dear God, thank You for making spiders. Amen.

Theme: Creation

#58

God Made Man

Materials: *paper and crayons*

"God created human beings in his image." Genesis 1:27.

[Illustrate this paragraph as you talk: beams, clouds, trees, etc.] On the first day of Creation God made light so we could see. On the second day God made air so we could breathe. On the third day God made plants so we could eat. On the fourth day God made the sun to keep us warm. On the fifth day God made birds to fill the air and fish to fill the water. On the sixth day God made animals to help us and keep us company.

The Bible says, "God looked at everything he had made, and it was very good" (Genesis 1:31). Everything was perfect. The world was ready for the next step: people.

When God made light, He said, "Let there be light!" And there it was. When God made plants, He said, "Let the earth produce plants." And it happened. But when God made the first man, it was different.

The Bible says, "God took dust from the ground and formed man from it. The Lord breathed the breath of life into the man's nose. And the man became a living person" (Genesis 2:7).

Do you know that man's name? It was Adam. God made Adam with His own hands. Adam was perfect, just like this new world was perfect.

Dear God, thank You for making Adam. Thank You for making me. Amen.

#59

Theme: Creation

God Made Woman

Materials: *different kinds of stuffed animals or pictures of animals*

"It is not good for the man to be alone." Genesis 2:18.

After God made Adam He gave him a job. God brought all the animals to Adam and asked him to give them names. That was a big job. Let's pretend that you are Adam, and we'll see if you can name the animals.

[Show your child different kinds of animals. Help your child call each animal by its correct name.]

That's kind of fun, isn't it? I think Adam probably liked it too. But after a while Adam noticed something. He saw that each animal had a mate—another animal that looked like it. Each of the animals had a partner to help it and keep it company.

Adam noticed that he didn't have a helper. Adam looked at all the animals and realized that none of them were like him.

God said, "It is not good for the man to be alone. I will make a helper who is right for him" (Genesis 2:18).

Adam went to sleep and God took a rib from Adam's body. God used the rib to make a woman. Do you know that woman's name? It was Eve. Eve was perfect, just like Adam.

Eve was Adam's wife, and Adam was Eve's husband. They weren't alone. They had each other.

Dear God, thank You for making Eve. Thank you for making me. Amen.

Theme: Creation/Marriage

#60

It Was Very Good

Materials: *a paper grocery bag, scissors, old magazines, glue*

"God looked at everything he had made, and it was very good." Genesis 1:31.

God showed Adam and Eve His perfect new world and told them He was giving it to them. He told them to take good care of it.

God had made Adam and Eve in His image. None of the other animals on earth had been made in God's image.

There was something else special about the humans. They could think and understand and make choices. Adam and Eve would be able to choose if they would follow God's plan.

The Bible says, "God blessed them and said, 'Have many children and grow in number. Fill the earth and be its master'" (Genesis 1:28).

That was God's plan. Adam and Eve would talk with the angels and walk with God. They would have lots of children, and everyone would be very happy.

At the end of the sixth day of Creation God looked at everything He had made, and it was very good.

[Make a "sixth day shirt." Cut along the center of the grocery bag. Cut a neck opening in the bag bottom and arm holes in each side. Cut pictures from magazines of things created on the sixth day. Glue them to the paper vest.]

Dear God, thank You for making everything so very good. Amen.

#61

Theme: Creation

God Made Sabbath

Materials: *fold a piece of paper in half, then in half again and again, so that there are eight sections when you unfold it; crayons or markers*

"In six days the Lord made everything. . . . And on the seventh day, he rested. Exodus 20:11.

On the first day of Creation God made light. *[In the first section of the paper, help your child draw beams of light.]* On the second day God made air. *[As you mention each day, illustrate the next section.]* On the third day God made the land and plants. On the fourth day God made the sun, moon, and stars. On the fifth day God made birds and fish. On the sixth day God made animals and humans.

There is one more day in Creation week. The seventh day. Do you know what God created on the seventh day? The Sabbath. *[In the seventh section draw a church.]*

The Bible says, "On the seventh day he rested from all his work. God blessed the seventh day and made it a holy day" (Genesis 2:2, 3).

The Sabbath is a day of rest. On Sabbath God quit working. He sat back and enjoyed the wonderful new world. He made friends with the new animals. He talked with Adam and Eve.

That first Sabbath was such a happy day. God decided that we should have a Sabbath every week so that we will always remember that God created our wonderful world. *[In the last section write "It was very good."]*

Dear God, thank you for creating Sabbath. Amen.

Theme: Creation

LLFJ-11

#62

Together

Activity: *guessing game*

"God blessed the seventh day and made it a holy day." Genesis 2:3.

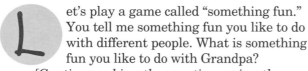

Let's play a game called "something fun." You tell me something fun you like to do with different people. What is something fun you like to do with Grandpa?

[Continue asking the question, using the names of different relatives and friends.]

Do you know something fun I like to do with you? Anything! I like to be with you. It is fun to spend time together.

When God created the world, He was pleased. He looked at everything He had made and it was very good. He especially loved the people he had made. He wanted to be with them. So God created one more thing: the Sabbath.

The seventh day of the week is Sabbath. God said Sabbath would be a special day. He blessed it and made it holy. God made Sabbath so we could spend time together.

You like to spend time with *[Grandpa]* and *[build things]*. I like to spend time with you and *[read stories]*. And God wants to spend time with you too. That's why He made the Sabbath.

Dear God, thank You for making Sabbath. Amen.

#63

Theme: The Sabbath

A Day of Rest

Materials: *seven pieces of paper with the days of the week written on them (write Sabbath instead of Saturday); juice or crackers (optional)*

"We may enter and have his rest."
Hebrews 4:1.

Look at these papers! They have the days of the week written on them. *[Together, say the days of the week in order.]*

Would you like to play a game with these papers? *[Have the child help you lay the papers on the floor in a line, with several inches between each paper.]*

First, let's practice. I'll count, and for every number I say, you will jump. *[Have the child practice jumping in place while you count to 10—sort of like jumping rope without the rope.]*

Now let's try jumping like that on each paper. We will pretend we are jumping through the week. First Sunday! *[Jump 10 times each on the Sunday through Friday papers. This should tire them out—you can adjust the number of jumps if you need to.]*

Whoa! Are you tired? Why don't we sit down on the Sabbath paper and take a little break. *[Perhaps you could offer juice or a cracker.]*

When God made the world, He knew that we couldn't work hard all the time. We need to rest. We need to catch our breath. God made Sabbath so we could take a break from our work each week. The Sabbath is a day of rest.

Dear Jesus, thank You for a chance to rest. Amen.

Theme: The Sabbath

#64

The Sabbath Law

Materials: *a pink piece of paper with "Good Advice" written on it; a red piece of paper with "The Law" written on it*

"Remember to keep the Sabbath as a holy day." Exodus 20:8.

D o you know the difference between good advice and the law? Let's play a game and find out. I will say an idea. If you think it is just good advice, hold up this piece of pink paper. If you think it is the law, hold up this red paper. Ready?

- Don't steal. *[Child holds up red paper. Discuss as needed.]*
- Wear a striped shirt. *[pink]*
- Tell the truth. *[red]*
- Stir your juice. *[pink]*
- Obey your parents. *[red]*
- Clap your hands. *[pink]*

All of these things are good, but some are more important than others. A friend may like your striped shirt, but you don't have to wear it if you don't want to. If you disobey Mom or Dad, however, it could lead to lots of unhappiness.

Here's one more question: The Sabbath—is it the law or just good advice? *[red paper]*

The Bible says it is the law. The Sabbath is one of the Ten Commandments, one of God's laws. The Sabbath is important. God wants us to keep the Sabbath holy.

Dear God, help me keep the Sabbath. Amen.

#65

Theme: The Sabbath

A Special Day

Materials: *paper, pencil, perhaps markers to decorate your poster*

"You should call the Sabbath a joyful day." Isaiah 58:13.

Sabbath is a special day. Special things happen. We can make plans to have a special Sabbath. Let's talk about things we could do to make this Sabbath special. *[Write your ideas on a paper or poster.]*

What can we do that would make Sabbath breakfast special? *[You can steer the ideas to be something along the line of "cinnamon toast cut into triangle shapes" rather than something complicated or stress-inducing.]*

What special clothes would you like to wear to church this Sabbath? *[The opportunity may arise to discuss why a pair of favorite nearly worn-out jeans may be special in their own way, but not right for church.]*

What special things do you think we will do at Sabbath school? What friends do you think we will see?

What special food could we have for Sabbath lunch? What could we do together on Sabbath afternoon that would be fun?

On Sabbath we get to go to church and worship God. We get to spend time with our family and friends. The Bible says that God has special blessings for us on Sabbath. Look at the wonderful day we have planned! Sabbath is a special day.

Dear God, thank You for Your Sabbath blessings. Amen.

Theme: The Sabbath

#66

The Sabbath Was Made for Us

Materials: *a jump rope [This activity could be modified to use with just about any toy.]*

"The Sabbath day was made to help people. They were not made to be ruled by the Sabbath day." Mark 2:27.

Let's say you want to jump rope. How would you feel if I kept telling you rules? *[Have the child try to jump while you constantly tell him to lift his feet higher, swing the rope harder, jump in rhythm, etc.]* It's not fun anymore, is it?

When Jesus was on earth, He kept the Sabbath. But there were some people who didn't think He kept it properly. The Jewish leaders had many rules about what people were allowed to do on Sabbath. These rules said that people should not carry things or cook or walk more than a few steps. There were lots of rules to remember.

One Sabbath Jesus and His disciples were walking by some fields. The disciples picked some grain and ate it while they walked along. Some Jewish leaders saw them do this and said the disciples had broken the Sabbath laws.

Jesus told the leaders that the Sabbath was made for people. People were not made to be ruled by the Sabbath. The rules were ruining the Sabbath blessings. People were so worried about keeping the rules that the Sabbath was not a day of joy. Jesus wants Sabbath to be a blessing.

Try jumping rope again, and I promise not to say a word!

Dear Jesus, help me to remember what Sabbath is for. Amen.

#67

Theme: The Sabbath

The Lying Snake

Activity: *nod or shake head*

"Lord, teach me what you want me to do.
And I will live by your truth." Psalm 86:11.

Lucifer had a new name—now he was called Satan. Satan was angry with God. He hated the new world. He hated all the happiness. He wanted to spoil it.

Adam and Eve had one test to show that they were choosing to follow God's rules. God put a tree in the middle of the garden and asked them not to eat the fruit from that tree.

That's where Satan decided to trick them.

One day Eve walked by the forbidden tree, and a snake called to her. She'd never heard an animal talk before. She didn't know the snake was really Satan in disguise. The snake was so charming and beautiful, and he had such interesting ideas.

I'll tell you some of the things the snake said. If it's the truth, say, "Yes, that's right." If you think the snake is telling a lie, say, "No, no, that isn't so." The snake said:

"If you eat this fruit, you'll gain more power."

"God doesn't want you to eat this because He doesn't want you to be as smart as He is."

"Of course you won't die if you eat it."

You said "No, no" every time, didn't you? Everything Satan said was a lie.

Dear God, I want to live by Your truth.
Amen.

Theme: The Great Controversy

 #68

Sin Leads to Death

Materials: *clear glass, cool water, red food coloring*

"When someone sins, he earns what sin pays—death." Romans 6:23.

Watch this glass of water. I am going to make it turn red. *[Add a drop to the water.]* Let's watch while I tell more of the story of Adam and Eve.

Satan, disguised as a snake, told Eve that she wouldn't die if she ate the fruit. And when she took a bite, she didn't die right away. When she took some to Adam and he took a bite, he didn't fall over dead, either. But that is when they started to die.

It's like when we put the drop of red in our glass of water. The water didn't turn red instantly. What is happening? *[It's swirling; spreading slowly.]* The water is not completely red yet, but it is starting to turn red.

When Adam and Eve chose to eat the fruit, they chose to disobey God. They sinned. That's when things started to go wrong. Sin entered this world, like the drop of red entered the water. Things were no longer perfect. Things began to go wrong.

When God came to see Adam and Eve, they said they were sorry and they would never disobey again. But it was too late. Sin was already there. They couldn't take it back, just as we can't take the red out of this water.

Dear Jesus, please save me from sin. Amen.

#69

Theme: The Great Controversy

Disconnected

Materials: *a dry leaf and a fresh leaf, or dry and fresh pine needles*

"It is your evil that has separated you from your God." Isaiah 59:2.

[G]o outside together to search for a dry leaf. Also pick a fresh leaf.] These leaves look different. This one is soft and green. This one is dry and brown. We picked this green one off the tree. In a few hours it will start to turn brown too. It is not connected to the tree anymore. It is starting to die. It reminds me of Adam and Eve.

When Adam and Eve chose to disobey God, they broke away from God. They were not connected anymore. Things started to change. Now Adam and Eve had to work hard to grow food to eat. They had to pull up the weeds that began to crowd out the good plants.

Now their animal friends were afraid of them. The animals stopped coming up for hugs and scratches behind the ears. Some of the animals turned fierce and began to eat other animals. It was very sad.

But the saddest thing of all was that Adam and Eve couldn't be with God anymore. Before they sinned, God would come to see them and they would go for walks together. Before they disobeyed, Adam and Eve had been able to talk with God, just like you and I talk. They were connected. But sin separated them from God.

Dear God, I want to be connected to You. Amen.

Theme: The Great Controversy

#70

A Plan to Save

Materials: *library books, a library card; take a trip to the library and check out some books*

"Christ Jesus came into the world to save sinners." 1 Timothy 1:15.

We borrowed these books from the library. We chose the books, then we took them to the desk to check them out. This is our library card. We showed our card and the librarian put this stamp on the book so we know when to bring it back.

If we forget to take the library books back on time, we will have to pay a fine. We have to pay money for every day the books are late. That is the penalty. Those are the rules.

When we have to pay a fine for overdue library books, it's not a very big penalty. There are much bigger penalties.

The penalty for sin is death. When Adam and Eve sinned, the penalty had to be paid. God loved Adam and Eve. He didn't want to lose them forever. That's why God the Father and God the Son had made a plan.

God the Son would pay the penalty for the people. He would take their place. He would die for their sins.

In this plan the people would be saved because a Redeemer would take their punishment. In this plan sin would be destroyed. In this plan someday there would be peace again in heaven and earth. It is a wonderful plan.

Dear God, thank You for Your plan to save me. Amen.

#71

Theme: The Great Controversy

God's Plan for Noah

Material: *a bath towel*

"But God remembered Noah and all the wild animals and the tame animals with him in the boat." Genesis 8:1.

God's plan to save the world didn't happen right away. It took thousands of years. Through all those years God told people about His plan to save them.

God had a special plan to save Noah and his family. By the time Noah was born, the sin that had begun with Adam and Eve had taken over the world. The people in the world were very wicked. God decided to send a flood to wash away the wickedness. God chose Noah to help Him because Noah was a good man.

God told Noah to build a big boat. Noah followed God's plan.

Then God sent animals to the boat. Let's pretend this towel is a ramp to the boat. I will say an animal, then you pretend to be that animal and go up the ramp into the boat. Here comes a kangaroo. The kangaroo hops into the boat. Look! A snake! The snake is wiggling up the ramp. Here's a lion. The lion looks very fierce! *[Continue as long as you want.]*

Now the animals are in the boat. Let's roll up the ramp and close the door. Noah will take care of the animals until the Flood is over.

During the Flood God took care of Noah and his family and the animals.

Dear God, thank You for taking care of Noah and the animals. Amen.

Theme: The Great Controversy

#72

God's Plan for Abraham

Materials: *six spoons, five pencils, four socks, a cup of sand, a piece of paper*

"I will make your descendants as many as the dust of the earth." Genesis 13:16.

After the Flood the earth began to fill up with people and animals again. God wanted them to know about His plan to save them. God chose Abraham to help Him. Abraham worshiped God. He was a good man. God told Abraham that He was going to bless him. People would see that Abraham was blessed because he worshiped God. Then people would want to find out about God.

God also promised Abraham that he would have many descendants—children and grandchildren and great-grandchildren. This was a wonderful promise. Abraham didn't have any children yet, but he wanted them more than anything.

Do you like to count? How many spoons are here? How many pencils? How many socks? You are a good counter. Now, how many grains of sand are here? *[Pour the sand onto a paper.]* We can't count this sand! It's too much!

God promised Abraham that he would have as many descendants as there are grains of sand on the earth. That's a lot of sand! That's a lot of descendents! God's plan was that Abraham and his family would tell others how much God loved them. We are Abraham's children, because we love God too and tell others about Him.

Dear God, I want to follow You like Abraham. Amen.

#73

Theme: The Great Controversy

It's Not Too Hard for God

Activity: *flying*

"Is anything too hard for the Lord? No!"
Genesis 18:14.

Wouldn't it be fun if we could fly? Let's pretend you're a bird. *[Pick your child up and zoom him / her around the room.]* That's fun! But people can't really fly, even though we wish we could.

There are lots of things people can't do. But nothing is too hard for God.

God promised Abraham he would have as many descendants as the sand. But Abraham and his wife, Sarah, were getting old and they still didn't have any children. Abraham began to wonder how God was going to keep His promise.

Then one day the Lord and two angels came by in disguise. Abraham gave them some lunch, and while they were eating, the Lord said that the next year Sarah would have a baby. Sarah was listening inside the tent, and she laughed because she knew she was too old to have a baby.

The Lord said, "Why did Sarah laugh? . . . Is anything too hard for the Lord?" (Genesis 18:13, 14). Nothing is too hard for God. Abraham and Sarah did have a baby, and they named him Isaac, which means "laughter." God keeps His promises.

God wanted the people to know about Him. We call the descendents of Abraham and Isaac the "Israelites." They became the people of God.

Dear God, it's good to know that nothing is too hard for You. Amen.

Theme: The Great Controversy

#74

God's Plan for Moses

Material: *an action figure or a picture / cartoon of a superhero*

"Moses had great power. He did wonderful things for all the Israelites to see." Deuteronomy 34:12.

Do you know who this is? It's *[Mighty Man]*. We say he's a superhero because he has unusual powers he uses to help people. He's just a regular person until someone needs help. Then he changes into a superhero.

Is there really a [Mighty Man]? No. He's just pretend. But there are heroes in the Bible who had some amazing powers. Their power came from God. And these stories are true!

Moses was just a quiet shepherd, watching his sheep, when God talked to him from a burning bush. God told Moses He wanted him to rescue the Israelites—the descendants of Abraham. The Israelites were being held as slaves by the Egyptians. Moses didn't want to do it. He had all kinds of excuses. He told God that he didn't know how to rescue anybody. He didn't know what to say.

Finally God got tired of the excuses. "Now go!" God said. "I will tell you what to say."

Moses obeyed. He got braver as he realized that God really was with him. The more he obeyed, the more he realized that nothing is impossible with God. Moses and God, working together, rescued the Israelites from slavery. Moses became a real superhero.

Dear God, I want to work with You as Moses did. Amen.

#75

Theme: The Great Controversy

God Gives the Rules

Activity: *discuss rules*

"We will do everything he has said."
Exodus 19:8.

I n our home we have some rules. Can you think of some? *[Don't hurt anyone; put away things when you are done using them; etc.]* What would our home be like if there were no rules? *[People might get hurt; our house would be cluttered; etc.]* How do the rules help everyone be happy? *[Help us get along, share, be safe, be kind, etc.]*

Rules help us. God gave us rules too.

One special time God talked to all of His people at once. He had just rescued them from Egypt. They were camped in the desert by a mountain.

The Israelites had been slaves for so long, many of them didn't know much about God.

They had forgotten the promises God made to Abraham. God wanted to tell them how to be His people. He wanted tell them how they could have happy lives.

Moses told the people to gather by the mountain. God came down in a thick cloud. There was thunder and lightning and fire. The mountain shook. Then God spoke. "I am the Lord your God."

The people paid attention. They listened while God gave them His commandments.

Dear God, thank You for giving us Your rules. Amen.

Theme: The Law of God

#76

Laws to Honor God

Materials: *eight pieces of paper, two pencils or markers*

"Love the Lord your God with all your heart, soul and strength."
Deuteronomy 6:5.

The first four commandments God gave His people were about how to honor God. *[Write a big number 1. Let your child make some 1's on another paper.]* God told His people, "You must not have any other gods except me" (Exodus 20:3). The Israelites needed to learn that there was only one God. The people of other nations had lots of gods they had made up themselves. God wants to make sure we know that He is the real God, the only God.

[Write a 2.] God said, "You must not make idols." It doesn't make sense for us to worship something we've made. We must worship God, who made us.

[Write a 3.] God said, "You must not use My name thoughtlessly." If we say God's name in a thoughtless way when we are surprised or angry, God becomes less special to us. God's name is holy. We must be careful when we say His name.

[Write a 4.] God said, "Remember to keep the Sabbath as a holy day" (verse 8). The Sabbath is a special gift. We get a little vacation each week to remember that God created us. On Sabbath we get a chance to learn more about God.

The first four commandments help us learn to love God.

Dear God, I want to learn to love and honor You. Amen.

#77

Theme: The Law of God

Honor Your Parents

Materials: *coupon-sized papers, markers or crayons, maybe some stickers*

"Children, obey your parents the way the Lord wants." Ephesians 6:1.

God wants His people to learn to love Him and each other. When God came to the mountain to talk to His people, He gave us commandments that show us how we should treat each other.

Commandment number 5 is about families. For families to be happy, there must be love at home. God told His people, "Honor your father and your mother" (Exodus 20:12). What do you think it means to honor your parents? *[Obey, respect, love.]*

When children honor their parents, everyone is happier. Instead of punishment, there is reward. Instead of worry, there is trust. Instead of scolding, there is laughing.

Think of ways you can show obedience, love, or respect. I will write the words on these little papers, and you can decorate them. Then you can give the coupons to me for a present; I will turn a coupon back when I need some honor. If you make a coupon that says "I will stop whining," whenever I give you the coupon you will stop whining. *[Suggestions: go to bed cheerfully, obey right away, a hug and a kiss.]*

I'll make some coupons for you to give me, too. *[Suggestions: a hug and a kiss, smile, sing a song, play a game with me, tell me a story.]*

Dear God, help me to honor my parents. Amen.

Theme: Christian Behavior

LLFJ-13

#78

Life Is Holy

Materials: *two dolls or action figures*

"Never shout angrily or say things to hurt others." Ephesians 4:31.

God's people were gathered by the mountain. God gave them more commandments that showed them how to love each other. Commandment number 6 is a very important rule about love.

God told His people, "Do not kill." God wants us to love each other, and of course that means we must not kill each other. God gave us life. Life is holy. We must not take it away from anyone.

Jesus says that this law also means that we must not get angry at each other or say bad things to each other (Matthew 5:21, 22).

When someone gets angry at you, does it make you feel sad? When someone says bad things to you, does it hurt your feelings? When someone is mean to us, it takes away the happiness of our life. Life is holy. We must not take the happiness away from anyone.

You hold one doll and I'll hold the other. Let's pretend that these dolls are playing. *[Act this out.]* Your doll accidentally breaks one of my doll's toys. My doll gets angry and yells at your doll. How does your doll feel? Do you think my doll disobeyed commandment number 6? What should my doll do now?

Dear Jesus, show me how to give happiness, not take it away. Amen.

#79

Theme: Christian Behavior

Happy, Happy Home

Materials: *wedding photos*

"Two people are better than one. They get more done by working together."
Ecclesiastes 4:9.

God was speaking to the Israelites from the cloud on the mountain. God gave the people His commandments. The people listened carefully as God told them the rules for living a happy life.

God wants us to have happy families. In commandment number 5 God says that children should honor their parents. Now, in commandment number 7, He says that husbands and wives should honor each other.

If a family is going to be strong and happy, the husband and wife must honor each other. How do they do that? They are loyal and stick up for each other. They support and encourage each other. They are nice to each other. They love each other.

When two people get married, they promise to love each other and be loyal to each other. They promise that they will stick together, in the good times and the bad times. They promise to take care of each other.

A wedding is a time to make promises. Would you like to see some pictures of a wedding? *[Talk about when and where the wedding took place, identify the people in the photos, talk about the special clothes and food, etc.]*

Dear God, help me to learn to keep my promises. Amen.

Theme: Christian Behavior

#80

Honesty Is the Best Policy

Materials: *a nice-looking toy, a beat-up toy; a whole cookie, a half-eaten cookie*

"Do what is right to other people."
Micah 6:8.

God gave the people His commandments. They show us how to be happy. Commandment number 8 is important if we want to get along with each other.

God tells His people, "You must not steal" (Exodus 20:15). That means you don't take things that don't belong to you.

You can't take someone else's toy and keep it. You shouldn't go to the neighbor's house and pick their flowers. You can't take things from the store without paying for them.

You mustn't take things that aren't yours. But this commandment means more than that. God wants us to be honest. If your friend has a toy that you like *[show nice toy]*, would it be right for you to talk him into trading it for this toy? *[Show beat-up toy.]* No, that wouldn't be honest.

God wants us to be fair. If you ate half of your cookie, would it be fair to trick your sister into trading her whole cookie? *[Show cookies.]* No, that wouldn't be fair.

God wants us to do our best. If I ask you to put away your toys, should you just stuff them under the bed? No, that wouldn't be right.

If we want to be happy, we'll be honest.
Dear God, please help me to be honest. Amen.

#81

Theme: Christian Behavior

Telling the Truth

Materials: *Before you tell this story, work together to make two paper bag puppets—a Mama Puppet and a Kid Puppet—out of lunch-size bags*

"Tell each other the truth because we all belong to each other." Ephesians 4:25.

G od spoke from the top of the mountain. He gave the Israelites His commandments. Commandment number 9 warns us not to tell lies. Telling lies causes trouble. Telling lies makes people unhappy.

What is a lie? Is it saying something that's not true? I'll say something, and you tell me if it's a lie:

The elephant said, "I like my new hat."

Can elephants talk? No! Do elephants wear hats? No! I was just making that up for fun. It's not true; it's pretend. When I pretend, am I telling a lie? No. It's not a lie as long as we both know it's just pretend.

A lie is trying to make someone believe something that is not true. A lie is trying to trick someone on purpose. Let's pretend that this kid puppet drew on the wall with crayons.

He can lie with words. Mama Puppet: "Did you draw on the wall?" Kid Puppet: "No."

He can lie with silence. MP: "Who drew on the wall?" KP: (nothing).

He can lie with actions. KP: "I'll put my brother's crayons here so Mom will think he did it."

Or he can tell the truth. KP: "I did it. I'm sorry. I'll clean it up."

Dear Jesus, help me always to tell the truth. Amen.

Theme: Christian Behavior

#82

Be Content

Purrrrrrr

Materials: *cotton balls, glue, a piece of paper with a cat shape drawn on it*

"Be satisfied with what you have."
Hebrews 13:5.

Some of God's commandments are about things we should not **do**. Some of them are about things we should not **say**. And the last one is about things we should not even **think!**

Commandment number 10 tells us it is important to be happy with what we have.

God says, "You must not want to take anything that belongs to your neighbor" (Exodus 20:17). He has already told us, in number 8, that we should not take it. Now He tells us that we should not even **want** to take it. God knows that we cannot be happy if we want things we can't have.

It doesn't make sense to worry about what you can't have. If you do that, you won't be able to enjoy the wonderful things you can have.

Have you ever heard a cat purr? A cat doesn't get upset if the cat next door has more cat toys or more expensive cat food. Cats are happy with what they have. That's why they purr.

Let's fluff these cotton balls and glue them on this paper in the shape of a cat. We'll hang it up, and every time we see it we can pat it and remember to be happy with what we have.

Dear God, thank You for all that I have. Amen.

Theme: Christian Behavior

Deliver This Message

Materials: *someone to whom the child can deliver a kiss—if no one else is around, it can be given to a pet or stuffed animal; paper and crayon*

"You must say everything I tell you to say." Jeremiah 1:7.

I have something I want to give to Daddy *[or other designated recipient]*. Will you take it to him? *[Give the child a kiss.]* Please take that kiss to Daddy for me. Thank you.

Come back and tell me about it. How did Daddy like the kiss I sent? Did you tell him it was from me? Did you have fun?

You were a good messenger. You gave Daddy my message. Would you like to do it again? This time I think I'll send a written message. *[Draw a heart on a piece of paper.]* Will you take this message to Daddy?

Sometimes God wants to send people a message. He chooses a messenger. He tells the messenger what to say. The messenger tells God's message.

We have a special name for these messengers from God: prophets. Sometimes prophets tell God's messages by speaking and preaching. Sometimes prophets write down God's messages. Many parts of the Bible were written by prophets.

God has sent many different kinds of messages, but all of them have one main idea: I love you. God wants us to know that He loves us.

Dear God, thank You for sending us messages. Amen.

Theme: The Gift of Prophecy

#84

Learn to Do Good

Materials: *two dolls, action figures, or stuffed animals; two (real or pretend) cookies*

"Stop doing wrong! Learn to do good."
Isaiah 1:16, 17.

L et's play a game with these dolls. We'll pretend they don't know how to behave. I will make them do something naughty, then you tell them what they should do.

[While you "move" the dolls and "talk" for them, have them get into an argument—then one doll hits the other doll.] Oh no! What happened? Tell these dolls what they did that was wrong. *[Fighting and hitting.]* Tell them what they need to do instead. *[Play nicely.]*

Would you like a turn? Here are two cookies. Show me a story about how these dolls won't share. Then I'll tell them what they should do.

[Help your child act out a "not willing to share" scenario with the dolls. Then lecture the dolls on the importance of learning to share.]

Sometimes God wants to tell people how they should behave. So He tells His prophets what to say. "God says, 'Stop doing wrong!'" the prophets tell the people. "God wants you to learn to do good."

Sometimes the people listen to the prophets' message and try to do good. Sometimes the people don't like what the prophets say. God tells the prophets to keep giving the people His message of love.

Dear God, I want to listen to God's messengers and obey. Amen.

#85

Theme: The Gift of Prophecy

Turn to Me

Activity: *step and turn in rhythm to memory verse*

"The prophets call them to turn to me."
Hosea 11:7.

Again and again God tells the prophets to tell the people how much He loves them. The prophets say to everyone who will listen: "God loves you." The prophets write and write: "God loves you."

Sometimes prophets write poems or songs about God's messages. Would you like to learn one now? Stand next to me. See if you can step when I step and turn when I turn.

Say (in **strong** rhythm)	Action
The **pro**phets	step
Call them	step
To **turn**	turn
To **me**	stop

[Repeat until both of you can step and turn in rhythm. Then encourage the child to say the verse with you while you step.]

God wants us to turn to Him. He wants us to turn to Him when we need help. He wants us to turn to Him when we have questions. He wants us to turn away from sin.

God wants us to follow His plan. The prophets call us to turn to God.

Dear God, I want to follow You. Amen.

Theme: The Gift of Prophecy

LLFJ-14

#86

Looking Forward

Materials: *baby pictures and recent photos of your child*

"Before the Lord God does anything, he tells his servants the prophets."
Amos 3:7.

S *how baby pictures.]* Do you know who this baby is? It's you! This is what you looked like when you were a baby. *[Show recent photos.]* Who is this? It's you, of course. This is what you look like now.

[Hold baby and recent photos side by side.] You look different now. You don't look like a baby anymore. This is what you looked like in the past. This is what you look like now.

Sometimes I wonder what you will look like when you are 10 years old. I can only guess. I can see what you looked like in the past. I can see what you look like now. But I can't see what you will look like in the future.

We can't see the future. But sometimes God wants to tell us about the future. Do you know who He gives His message to? A prophet. God tells the prophet about the future, and the prophet tells us.

Many years ago the prophets said that a Redeemer would come to save us from our sins. And it happened! God sent Jesus—just as He promised.

The prophets say that Jesus will come again to take us to heaven. And He will! That's our future. That's a promise.

Dear God, thank You for telling us about the future. Amen.

#87

Theme: The Gift of Prophecy

A Light in a Dark Place

Materials: *a night-light; a piece of paper with a heart drawn on it; a place that can be fully darkened—e.g., an interior bathroom or a closet; a place to plug the night-light in (extension cord)*

"Their message is like a light shining in a dark place." 2 Peter 1:19.

Show night-light.] What's this? The night-light helps us see if we wake up in the night. We need light to see.

[Take the night-light into the bathroom or closet.] It's dark in here, isn't it? *[Hold up the heart paper.]* I'm holding up a paper with a message on it. Can you see what the message is? It's too dark! Let's turn on our night-light and see if that helps. Can you see the message now? What shape is drawn on the paper? What do you think my message is? I love you! *[You can come out now.]*

The prophets are like a light. They help us see what God wants to tell us. The Bible says, "Their message is like a light shining in a dark place."

About 100 years ago God sent messages to another prophet. God had many things He wanted to tell us. He chose a woman to be His prophet—her name was Ellen White. He gave her His messages and she wrote them down. She wrote books and preached sermons, telling people God's messages.

These messages are like a light. They help us understand the Bible. They help us know how God wants us to live. They tell us that God loves us.

Dear God, thank You for sending us messages. Help me to listen. Amen.

Theme: The Gift of Prophecy

#88

God's Plan for Samuel

Activity: *act out the story*

"Speak, Lord. I am your servant, and I am listening." 1 Samuel 3:10.

God made an agreement with the Israelites that they would be His people. They would tell other people about God and His plan to save them. Sometimes the Israelites did a good job, and sometimes they didn't.

God often chose a special helper to give the Israelites His messages. These helpers were called prophets. One of these prophets was Samuel. God chose Samuel when he was just a little boy.

Let's act out this story. You be Samuel and I'll be Eli the priest. You work for me in the temple.

Samuel, the tabernacle furniture needs to be dusted. *[Pause to let your child act this out.]* Sweep the floor, please. Now light the special candles. OK, Samuel, it's time to go to bed.

[Read from the Bible, 1 Samuel 3:2-10. Have your child lay down in "bed" and jump up and run to you at the appropriate times. Read Eli's words in a quavery old voice. Read the Lord's words in a deep solemn voice. After you read Samuel's words, pause to let your child repeat them.]

Samuel listened to God and told the people God's messages. Samuel was God's prophet all of his life.

Dear God, I will listen to You. Amen.

#89

Theme: The Great Controversy

God's Plan for David

Materials: *a glass of water or juice, filled half full, for everyone*

"You give me more than I can hold."
Psalm 23:5.

The Israelites were supposed to be good examples. They were supposed to show other nations how God wanted them to live. But sometimes the Israelites did just the opposite. Instead of being good examples to others, they followed other people's bad example.

The other nations had kings, so the Israelites decided they wanted a king too. Many of the Israelite kings did not lead the people wisely. But some kings were good, and they helped the Israelites be good examples.

David was a good king. David was an optimist. See this glass of water? Some people look at it and think it is half empty. Some people think it is half full. If you think it is half full, then we say you are an optimist. You don't worry about how much is gone. You are happy about how much is there.

David was an optimist. When he was just a boy, he knew that with God's help, he could kill a giant. And he did it. When he became king, he knew God would help him solve problems and win battles. David was a good example.

If David saw this glass of water, he would grab it, drink it down, and praise God for how good it was. We can do that too!

Dear God, thank You for giving me so much. Amen.

Theme: The Great Controversy

#90

Devotion

God's Plan for Jeremiah

Material: *clay or play dough*

"I will put my teachings in their minds. And I will write them on their hearts." Jeremiah 31:33.

God asked Jeremiah to be a prophet. Jeremiah was shy; he couldn't imagine being a prophet. But God said, "Don't be afraid. I am with you." God gently touched Jeremiah's mouth and said, "See, I am putting my words in your mouth" (Jeremiah 1:9).

Jeremiah obeyed. God made him strong. Whatever God told him to say, he said. And it usually got him into trouble. The people didn't like what Jeremiah told them. He told them that only God's power kept their enemies away. He warned them that terrible things would happen if they didn't follow God's plan.

God told Jeremiah to watch a man make pots out of clay. *[Illustrate with clay as you talk.]* When the pot didn't turn out right, did the potter throw the clay away? No. He just squashed it and started over. Jeremiah told the people that if they didn't follow God's plan, God would have to start over and reshape them—just like the clay. And that's what happened. The people wouldn't listen to Jeremiah. They wouldn't obey God. The enemy came and destroyed their city and took the people away as captives. God had to reshape the clay.

[Make heart shapes out of clay while you say the memory verse.]

Dear God, please write Your teachings on my heart. Amen.

#91

Theme: The Great Controversy

God's Plan for Daniel

Materials: *crayons, paper, a butter knife*

"He gives wisdom to people so they become wise." Daniel 2:21.

L et's make a scratch-off picture. *[Cover a piece of paper with bright crayons. Press hard and lay the colors on thick. Then color over the entire paper with black crayon.]*

Things looked dark for the Israelites. They had been captured. They were taken to Babylon. But God still watched over them. God chose Daniel to tell them about His plan.

The king of Babylon chose Daniel to be one of his servants. More than once Daniel had to chose whether to obey the king or obey God. He knew it was better to obey God, and God always took care of him. The king saw that Daniel al-ways did the right thing and gave wise advice. The king learned to respect Daniel's God.

God gave Daniel dreams that showed the future. Someday His people would go back to their country. *[Use a butter knife to scrape the black crayon—scratch out pictures of trees, houses, etc.]* Things wouldn't always be dark. Daniel's dreams showed the brightness behind the darkness, just like this picture. God showed Daniel that He hadn't forgotten His promise. Someday God would send a Redeemer to take the punishment for their sins. That was still God's plan.

Dear God, help me do the right thing, as Daniel did. Amen.

Theme: The Great Controversy

#92

God's Plan for Zerubbabel

Materials: *four pieces of paper, a marker, a heavy book*

"The power will come from my Spirit."
Zechariah 4:6.

While God's people were captives, they began to listen to the prophets. Finally the king said they could go back home. He chose Zerubbabel to lead them home. When the people reached Jerusalem, they saw that the city had been destroyed. That was a problem. *[Write "city destroyed" on a paper and loosely crumple it up.]* They started to rebuild the Temple. When the foundation was finished, they had a celebration. Some of the old people cried because this Temple wasn't as beautiful as the old one that had been destroyed. That was a problem. *[Write "crying" and crumple it.]*

Other people had moved into the country while the Jews were gone. They began to cause trouble. That was a problem. *[Write "trouble-makers" and crumple.]* A new king gave them an order to stop building. That was a problem. *[Write "orders" and crumple.]*

Poor Zerubbabel! It seemed as if he had a whole mountain of problems. *[Pile the papers into a mountain.]* God sent a message: "No mountain can stand in Zerubbabel's way!" And God's power flattened that mountain of problems. *[Squash the papers with the book.]* God's people rebuilt the Temple.

Dear God, send Your power to help me flatten my problems. Amen.

Theme: The Great Controversy

God's Plan for John

Materials: *a sandbox, toy trucks to flatten hills, cars to drive on the road. (If you don't have sand, you make hills with a big towel instead.)*

"Every mountain and hill should be made flat." Isaiah 40:4.

God needed a prophet to tell the people to get ready. Most people thought God was going to send a Redeemer to rescue them **from their enemies.** They'd forgotten God was going to rescue them from their sins.

Long ago the prophet Isaiah had written that God would send someone to prepare the way. *[Make hills in the sand.]* People's ideas were confused. Someone needed to smooth out the hills and bumps. *[Flatten the hills; make a level road.]* Then people could understand.

God chose John to help—before he was even born! An angel told Zechariah that they would have a baby named John who would grow up to "make people ready for the coming of the Lord" (Luke 1:17). Zechariah was surprised. He said, "Are you sure?" The angel said, "Yes, I'm sure. And because you didn't believe me you won't be able to talk."

After the baby was born, the relatives said he should be named after his father, but Zechariah shook his head and wrote, "His name is John." *[Write in the sand.]* Then Zechariah could talk again, so he gave a long speech—John was going to prepare the way for the coming of the Lord.

Dear Jesus, help me prepare the way for Your coming too. Amen.

Theme: Christ's Mission

LLFJ-15

#94

Angels Tell About God's Plan

Materials: *make an angel chain: cut a paper lengthwise; tape together; fold into eighths; draw angel shape (connect tips of the wings and bottom edges of skirt); cut out shape. A Nativity set or picture.*

"I am bringing you some good news."
Luke 2:10.

The angels were excited. It was time for Jesus to go to earth. The angel Gabriel was chosen to go tell Mary that she was going to be Jesus' mother. *[Hold up the still-folded angel cutout.]* Mary was startled. She had never seen an angel before. Gabriel whispered, "Don't be afraid, Mary." Then he announced, "Listen! You will have a baby and you'll name him Jesus.

Then Gabriel went to see Joseph. He told him that Jesus was going to save people from sin. Joseph promised to take care of Mary and the new baby.

Just before the baby was born, Joseph and Mary had to travel to Bethlehem. There was no place to stay, so they had to sleep in a stable. Jesus was born in that stable.

The angels were so happy they had to tell somebody. Some shepherds were in a field nearby. An angel appeared in front of them and said, "I have good news. Your Saviour has been born." Then a large group of angels appeared *[unfold the angel cutout]* and sang, "Glory to God!"

The shepherds found the stable. And this is what we think the first Christmas might have looked like. *[Arrange nativity set together.]*

Dear God, thank You for sending Baby Jesus. Amen.

#95

Theme: Christ's Mission

Jesus Learns About God's Plan

Materials: *three or more dolls or action figures*

"People liked him, and he pleased God."
Luke 2:52.

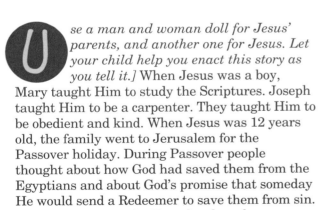

se a man and woman doll for Jesus' parents, and another one for Jesus. Let your child help you enact this story as you tell it.] When Jesus was a boy, Mary taught Him to study the Scriptures. Joseph taught Him to be a carpenter. They taught Him to be obedient and kind. When Jesus was 12 years old, the family went to Jerusalem for the Passover holiday. During Passover people thought about how God had saved them from the Egyptians and about God's promise that someday He would send a Redeemer to save them from sin.

Jesus went to the Temple where boys were being taught about God. He came in and listened. Then He asked a question. The teachers were amazed—it was a very good question. Soon the teachers began asking Him questions.

Mary and Joseph had already started for home. When they realized Jesus wasn't with them, they raced back to Jerusalem. Let's pretend this doll is Jesus. I'll hide Him in the next room. Then you try to find Him. Mary and Joseph found Jesus in the Temple. When Mary told Him they'd been worried about Him, Jesus said, "I'm working for My Father." Jesus realized He was God's Son. He knew what His Father wanted Him to do.

Dear God, teach me what You want me to do. Amen.

Theme: Christ's Mission

Jesus Accepts God's Plan

Materials: *paper, blue fingerpaint, papers cut in the shape of Jesus and a dove*

"This is my Son and I love him. I am very pleased with him." Matthew 3:17.

John was preparing the way, just as the angel had said he would. John told everyone who would listen that they were sinners and needed to repent. Lots of people were listening; they were lining up to be baptized in the river. John baptized them to show they were sorry for their sins.

Jesus heard about John and knew it was time to begin God's plan. He went to the river to be baptized. When John saw Jesus, he knew this was the Person for whom he had been preparing the way. "I can't baptize You," John said. "You should baptize me." How could he baptize someone who had never sinned?

But baptism means more than being sorry for sins. It also shows that you are choosing God. Jesus wanted to be baptized to show that He was accepting God's plan. Jesus said, "This is the right thing to do."

As John baptized Jesus in the river, the Holy Spirit took the shape of a dove and glided down from heaven, resting on Jesus. God said, "This is my Son and I love him."

Jesus chose God's plan, and God was pleased. Let's make a picture of this story.
[Fingerpaint with blue. While the paint is still wet, stick on paper cutouts of Jesus and a dove.]
Dear God, I want to follow Your plan. Amen.

#97

Theme: Baptism

Satan Tries to Trick Jesus

Materials: *paper or cardboard tube or popsicle stick, marker, glue or stapler*

"Go away from me, Satan!"
Matthew 4:10.

Help your child cut out a stop sign shape and write "NO" on it. Glue it on the tube. During the story the child holds up the sign and says "No" whenever you ask a question.] After He was baptized, Jesus needed to think. He went to the desert so He could be alone with His Father to talk about His plan. Jesus wanted to follow God's plan. For 40 days the only thing Jesus did was to pray. He was weak and hungry. Satan decided to try and trick Jesus.

Satan said, "If you are the Son of God, tell these rocks to become bread" (Matthew 4:3). What did Jesus say to Satan? *[Child holds up sign and says "no."]*

Satan took Jesus to the top of the Temple. He said, "If you are the Son of God, jump off and let the angels catch you" (see verse 6). What did Jesus say to Satan? *[No.]*

Satan showed Jesus all the world. He said, "If you will bow down and worship me, I will give you all these things" (verse 9). What did Jesus say to Satan? *[No.]*

Satan wanted Jesus to do wrong instead of follow God's plan. But Jesus said "no" to Satan. When Satan tries to get you to do the wrong thing, what can you say?

Dear Jesus, help me say "No" to Satan. Amen.

Theme: Christ's Mission

#98

Jesus Tells About God's Plan

Materials: *a handful of coins*

"My Temple will be a house where people will pray." Matthew 21:13.

Jesus went to Jerusalem for the Passover celebration. Lots of people were at the Temple. It was very noisy.

The people brought money for offerings. But they couldn't give just any money; they had to give the Temple shekel. So people traded their regular money for Temple money at the moneychanging tables. *[Jingle coins.]* The people wanted to give animals for offerings, so lots of animals were for sale. There were cows [moo], sheep, [baa], and pigeons [coo]. And men were calling and bargaining ["Sheep for sale"].

Jesus heard the noise. He saw cheating and stealing. It was a mess. He wanted to clean it up.

He turned over the tables. *[Knock something over.]* Money scattered everywhere. *[Scatter your coins.]* That got everyone's attention. "Take these things out of here! Don't make my Father's house a place for buying and selling!" Jesus commanded (John 2:16). All the shopkeepers and moneymakers ran away.

But the people who wanted to hear about God's love didn't run away. The children climbed on Jesus' lap. He told them stories. They sang songs for Him. *[Sing.]* Jesus healed people who were sick. Jesus told the people about God's plan.

Dear Jesus, help me to praise and honor God in church. Amen.

#99

Theme: Christ's Mission

A Good Example

Activity: *thinking of ways to serve and show love*

"Love each other as I have loved you."
John 15:12.

For three years Jesus taught about God's plan. Now Jesus knew it was time for Him to take the punishment for our sins. Jesus gathered His disciples for one last supper together.

In those days people wore sandals, and their feet got dirty. Usually a servant washed the feet of guests. There was no servant at this supper. One of the disciples should have offered to wash everyone's feet, but nobody wanted to. They thought they were too important to do a servant's work.

So Jesus did the servant's job. He washed their feet. He showed them that serving others is the most important kind of work. When He was done He said, "I did this as an example for you" (John 13:15). Jesus wants us to serve others. *[Together think of a way you could serve someone today.]*

During supper, Jesus talked to His disciples. He told them He was going to go away. He told them He would come back to take them to heaven. He promised to send the Holy Spirit to help them.

And He gave them one last command: "Love each other as I have loved you." Jesus loves us so much. He wants us to love others. *[Together think of a way you could show your love to others.]*

Dear Jesus, I want to follow Your example and serve others. Amen.

Theme: The Lord's Supper

#100

New Symbols

Materials: *pencil and paper*

"This bread is my body that I am giving for you." Luke 22:19.

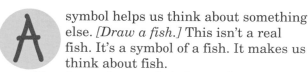 symbol helps us think about something else. *[Draw a fish.]* This isn't a real fish. It's a symbol of a fish. It makes us think about fish.

Here is another symbol. *[Draw $.]* What does that make you think of? *[Continue with other symbols, e.g., a flag, a cross, the sign indicating the men's or women's restroom.]*

The disciples understood about symbols. They had celebrated Passover every year. Passover had lots of symbols. At His last supper with the disciples, Jesus showed them some new symbols.

The Passover bread was a symbol of when God rescued the Israelites from slavery in Egypt. Jesus picked up the bread and gave each disciple a piece. Jesus told them that from now on the bread would be a symbol for His death. Jesus would die to rescue them from sin.

The Passover wine was a symbol to help the Israelites remember their freedom from slavery in Egypt. Jesus told His disciples that from now on it would help them remember that they were free from the slavery of sin.

In just a few hours Jesus was going to take the punishment for sin. He gave His followers some new symbols to remember this.

Dear Jesus, help me to remember that You took the punishment for my sins. Amen.

#101

Theme: The Lord's Supper

To Remember Me

Materials: *basin, water, towel, cracker, grape juice*

"Do this to remember me."
1 Corinthians 11:24.

At the Last Supper Jesus had with his disciples, He gave them some new symbols. He said the bread and wine would remind us that He died for our sins. As He gave the bread and wine to His disciples, He told them, "Do this to remember Me."

And that's what we do. Christians have a kind of worship called Communion. Communion means being together and sharing. When we have Communion together, we remember what Jesus did for us.

At a Communion service people take a bowl of water and a towel. *[Show.]* They find a partner. One person kneels down and washes their partner's feet. Then they trade places. We don't wash each other's feet because our feet are dirty. We do it to remember that Jesus wants us to serve each other.

At Communion we eat a small piece of Communion bread. *[Show.]* We don't eat the cracker because we are hungry. We eat it to remember that Jesus took the punishment for our sins.

At Communion we drink a little cup of grape juice. *[Show.]* We don't drink the juice because we are thirsty. We drink it to remember that Jesus set us free. We do this to remember Jesus.

Dear Jesus, I want to always remember what You did for me. Amen.

Theme: The Lord's Supper
LLFJ-16

#102

Jesus Fulfills God's Plan

Materials: *paper, crayons, black tempera paint, paintbrush*

"The punishment, which made us well, was given to him." Isaiah 53:5.

After that Last Supper Jesus went to a garden to pray. The Jewish leaders came and took Him to the high priest's house. They were jealous. They wanted to find something He had done wrong so they could get rid of Him. Finally the high priest asked, "Are you the Son of God?" Jesus answered, "Yes, I am" (Matthew 26:64). Everyone got angry and said that Jesus was telling lies and should be killed.

They took Jesus to Pilate, the Roman leader. Pilate couldn't find anything wrong with Jesus. But the crowd shouted that Jesus must die. "Their yelling became so loud that Pilate decided to give them what they wanted" (Luke 23:23, 24).

They took Jesus outside the city. They put Him on a cross. Even though it was the middle of the day, it got dark. Satan did not want Jesus to die for our sins. He tried to get Jesus to give up. He tried to get Jesus to come down off the cross. But Jesus knew that He was following God's plan.

Jesus said, "It is finished." Then He bowed His head and died. Jesus took the punishment for our sins. *[Draw a crayon picture of a hill with three crosses. Paint over it with black tempera thinned with water.]*

Dear Jesus, thank You for taking the punishment for my sins. Amen.

#103

Theme: Christ's Mission

Jesus Is Alive

Matérials: *paper, crayons, glue, glitter, tinfoil, tape*

"He is not here. He has risen from death as he said he would." Matthew 28:6.

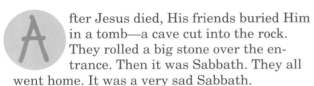fter Jesus died, His friends buried Him in a tomb—a cave cut into the rock. They rolled a big stone over the entrance. Then it was Sabbath. They all went home. It was a very sad Sabbath.

But Jesus was the Son of God. He couldn't stay dead. Very early Sunday morning, while it was still dark, there was an earthquake. An angel rolled the stone away from the tomb. Even though the sun wasn't up yet, it got very, very bright.

Jesus was alive.

Some women came to visit the tomb. They saw the stone was rolled away. They saw the angel, shining and bright. The angel said, "He is not here. He has risen from death as he said he would." The angel told them to go tell Jesus' friends, so they ran and told the others, "Jesus is alive!"

[Make a picture of light to contrast with yesterday's dark picture. Draw an outline of the tomb. Around it glue streams of light: glitter, strips of yellow paper, tinfoil. Make a stone door out of paper. Put it over the tomb entrance with a tape hinge. Lift the door, and under it write "He is not here."]

Dear Jesus, I am so glad You are alive. Amen.

Theme: Christ's Mission

#104

Jesus Gives Us a Job

Activity: *discuss ways to show God's love*

"Tell the Good News to everyone."
Mark 16:15.

During the 40 days after Jesus rose from death, He came to see His disciples several times. He helped them understand what had happened. He explained what was going to happen next.

Jesus said that He was going back to heaven, but He promised He would send a Helper—the Holy Spirit. The Holy Spirit would give them power. Why would they need power? Jesus had a job for His followers.

Jesus told them, "Go everywhere in the world. Tell the Good News to everyone" (Mark 16:15).

That is our job. God wants everyone to know how much He loves them. We can help. We can show people that God loves them. This is a big job. But Jesus will help us. Jesus said, "You can be sure that I will be with you always" (Matthew 28:20). After Jesus said this, He raised His hands and blessed His friends. Then He started to rise into the sky. He went higher and higher until He was hidden in the clouds.

Jesus' time on earth was over. The Son of God had gone back to His Father. Now His followers needed to begin their work. *[Talk about ways you can tell the Good News.]*

Dear Jesus, please help me show others how much You love them. Amen.

#105

Theme: The Church

God's Plan for Peter

Materials: *a small sheet or big towel; lots of stuffed animals*

"You are all the same in Christ Jesus."
Galatians 3:28.

Peter heard Jesus say, "Tell others the good news." Peter traveled from town to town preaching the good news about Jesus. But he was preaching only to the Jews. God wanted to teach Peter that everyone needed to hear about Jesus—not just the Jews. God sent Peter a dream.

In this dream a big sheet full of all kinds of animals came down from heaven. *[Enact.]* Peter heard a voice say, "Get up and eat."

The Jews had strict laws about food. They could eat only certain kinds of animals. The animals in this dream were not the kind they would eat. Peter said, "No!"

The voice said, "God has made these things clean" (Acts 10:15). Then it all happened again and again. *[Repeat twice more.]* Peter was confused by this dream. What could it mean? Just then some men knocked at the gate. They wanted Peter to come see their friend Cornelius. An angel had told Cornelius to send for Peter.

Then Peter realized what his dream meant. Cornelius was not a Jew. The animals in the dream were symbols for the non-Jews. God wanted Peter to preach to everyone. From then on, that's what Peter did.

Dear God, I am glad that Your good news is for everyone. Amen.

Theme: The Church

#106

Devotion

Paul Is Converted

Materials: *socks and T-shirts; ingredients to make cookie or bread dough*

"If anyone belongs to Christ, then he is made new." 2 Corinthians 5:17.

Paul thought Jesus' followers, the Christians, were causing trouble. He tried to destroy the new church by putting Christians in jail. Paul decided to go to Damascus and arrest those Christians. Suddenly a bright light flashed. Paul fell to the ground. He heard a voice say, "Why are you doing things against me?" (Acts 9:4). The light was so bright Paul couldn't see who was talking. He asked, "Who are you?"

The voice answered, "I am Jesus. I am the One you are trying to hurt" (verse 5). Then Paul was sorry for trying to hurt the Christians who were following Jesus. Jesus told him, "I want you on My side, Paul." And Paul was changed. Instead of working against Jesus, he wanted to work for Jesus.

You can mix some things together *[mix socks and shirts]* and then take them apart again *[separate them]*. The socks and shirts didn't change. But other things change when you mix them together. When we mix the ingredients for cookies, they are converted into something else. The flour and eggs and sugar become dough. Paul was converted—like the dough. He became a different kind of person. *[Make cookies or bread.]*

Dear Jesus, change me to be more like You. Amen.

Theme: Salvation

Paul Is Baptized

Materials: *honey, dirt, soap, and warm water*

"Be baptized, and wash your sins away." Acts 22:16.

After Paul was converted, he thought about the horrible things he had done. He wondered why Jesus had chosen him. He prayed, telling Jesus that from now on he would follow God's plan.

Jesus told a man named Ananias to go see Paul. Ananias told Paul that God had chosen him to tell other people about Jesus. Then Ananias said, "Be baptized, and wash your sins away."

Paul was baptized to show that he was choosing to follow God's plan. Paul was baptized to show that he was sorry for his sins and didn't want to sin any more. Paul wanted to wash his sins away.

Let's see how dirty we can get your hands. First let's spread some honey on your hands. Then let's rub them in the dirt. Yuck! That's terrible! Let's go wash this dirt away.

When someone is baptized, does the **water** wash the sins away—like the water washes the dirt off our hands? No. Only Jesus can take our sins away. The water is a symbol. When we are baptized, it shows that we believe Jesus has taken our sins away. It shows that we want to follow God's plan.

Dear Jesus, thank You for washing our sins away. Amen.

Theme: Baptism

#108

God's Plan for Paul

Materials: *lots of pennies*

"Because we loved you, we were happy to share God's Good News with you."
1 Thessalonians 2:8.

P aul began to work hard for Jesus. He traveled from city to city, telling everyone who would listen the good news about Jesus. Paul became a missionary.

When Paul went to a new city, first he went to the Jewish meetings on Sabbath. He would begin preaching about God's plan to save His people. He would teach that Jesus was God's Son, and that He died for our sins. Usually some people would be interested and would ask Paul to tell them more.

Before too long, the Jewish leaders would get upset. Many times they would cause so much trouble Paul would have to leave town.

But he usually managed to tell some of the people the good news before he had to leave. Those people would start a church and begin telling others about Jesus. And that's how the good news about Jesus began to spread.

Let's pretend this penny is Paul. Paul goes to a city and tells two people about Jesus. *[Put two pennies in a row beneath Paul's penny.]* Those two people each tell two people. *[Put down four more pennies. Continue until you run out of pennies or patience.]* See how quickly the good news can spread!

Dear Jesus, I want to help spread the good news about Jesus.

#109

Theme: The Church's Mission

God's Plan for You

Materials: *superhero figure, sand, glass of water, artwork from past devotionals*

"Your plans for us are many." Psalm 40:5.

When God created our world, there was a plan. God planned for everything to be good and everyone to be happy. When Adam and Eve disobeyed, God had a plan to make the world good again—God the Son would take our punishment for us. When Jesus came to earth to die for our sins, He was following God's plan. From the beginning, God has wanted to tell us about His plan to make us happy. He has always wanted to tell us how much He loves us. *[Choose to review some or all of the following.]*

God had a plan for Noah. Do you remember when you pretended to be a kangaroo hopping into the ark? *[Reenact.]* God had a plan for Abraham. Remember all the sand? God had a plan for Moses. *[Show superhero.]* He became a great leader! God had a plan for Samuel. Do you remember what Samuel answered when God called him? God had a plan for David. Would David think this glass was half full or half empty? *[Continue in the same manner for Jeremiah / clay; Daniel / scratch picture; Zerubbabel / paper mountain; John / flattening hills; Jesus / dark picture, light picture; Peter / animals; Paul / dough.]* And God has a plan for you. God wants you to know how much He loves you. God wants you to follow His plan.

Dear God, I want to follow Your plan.

Theme: The Great Controversy

#110

God Wants You to Be Happy

Materials: *paper, crayons, magazines, scissors, glue, stapler, optional picture of Jesus with children*

"Being with you will fill me with joy." Psalm 16:11.

When God created the world, He filled it with everything we would ever need, and it was very good. But even if we have every good thing in the world, that is not all we need to be happy. *[Make a book called "Happiness Is . . ." with at least four pages that show things that make us happy (e.g., puppies, strawberries, swimming, new shoes). Draw pictures or cut pictures out of magazines.]*

God gave us the law. The law tells us how we should live. The law tells us what we should do to be happy. But even if we could keep every law there ever was, that is not all we need to be happy. *[Make at least four pages that show rules that help keep us happy (e.g., share, take turns, say please, obey).]*

We need more than things. We need more than rules. We need to know God. Happiness is being friends with God. Happiness is knowing how much God loves us. God wants you to be happy. God wants to be friends with you.

[The last page says, "Happiness is being friends with God." If you have one, glue on a picture of Jesus with children. Staple the pages into a book.]

Dear God, I want to be friends with You. Amen.

#111

Theme: The Great Controversy

God Wants You to Love Yourself

Materials: *stuffed animals*

"You are worth much more than many sparrows." Luke 12:7.

Someone asked Jesus who was most important in the kingdom of heaven. Jesus called a little child to come to Him. He said that everyone needs to become more like little children. Children are important to Jesus.

Then He told a story about a lost sheep. Would you like to act it out while I read it? *[Hide one stuffed animal. Put a bunch more together in a group. Read Matthew 18:12-14 while your child acts it out. Pause to allow time to find the lost sheep.]*

In this story Jesus is the shepherd and you are the lost sheep. Jesus searched for you. Jesus loves you. You are His wonderful, valuable, one-of-a-kind lamb. You are worth so much that Jesus paid for you with His life. You are special. No one else looks exactly like you. No one else acts exactly like you. No one can replace you.

It is important for you to remember that you are valuable. When you do, we say that you love yourself.

You can't be happy if you don't love yourself. God wants you to be happy. He wants you to know how much you are worth. He wants you to love yourself.

Dear Jesus, help me remember that I am Your valuable, special child. Amen.

Theme: The Great Controversy

#112

Devotion

God Wants You to Love Your Family

Materials: *paper, pencil, family photos*

"If one person falls, the other can help him up." Ecclesiastes 4:10.

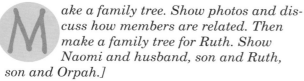ake a family tree. Show photos and discuss how members are related. Then make a family tree for Ruth. Show Naomi and husband, son and Ruth, son and Orpah.]

There was a famine, so Naomi and her husband went to Moab. Their sons married girls from Moab—Ruth and Orpah. Naomi's husband and sons died, so she decided to go back to Israel. Ruth went with Naomi. Ruth had learned about God, and she didn't want to go back to her old life.

They needed food, so Ruth went to a field to pick up leftover grain. The field belonged to Boaz. He was nice to Ruth. Naomi thought it would be good for Ruth and Boaz to get married. Boaz and Ruth liked that idea, too, because that's what they did. *[Add Boaz to family tree.]* They had a baby named Obed *[add to tree]*.

Ruth was a valuable member of her family. She loved Naomi, and helped her. She loved Boaz, too. She made a difference. You are a valuable part of your family. You can make a difference. The things you do can make your home a happier place. You can be kind. You can be thoughtful. You can be helpful.

Families take care of each other. God gave us families because He wants us to be happy.

Dear God, thank You for my family. Amen.

Theme: Christian Behavior

God Wants You to Love Your Enemies

Materials: *clay, uncooked spaghetti*

"But I tell you, love your enemies. Pray for those who hurt you." Matthew 5:44.

M ake a porcupine body out of clay. Break spaghetti into pieces and poke them into the clay.]
    A porcupine is prickly. Its fur has strong quills that are extremely sharp. If an enemy tries to bite a porcupine, the quills leave the porcupine and stick into the enemy. Ouch! The enemy runs away.

Sometimes we say a person is prickly. We mean they are unfriendly. People don't have quills—they show prickliness by being rude or selfish or mean. What should you do with a prickly person?

Jesus says you should love them. How can you do that?

You can't love a prickly person the same way you love your family. The love you have for your family is a cozy, warm feeling. But you can't force yourself to have this feeling. You can't force yourself to love a prickly person this way.

Jesus gives us another kind of love. This kind of love makes us willing to treat people right—even when they don't like us and we don't particularly like them. With this kind of love, we can treat everyone with kindness, even if they aren't nice to us.

Jesus will help you love your enemies.

Dear Jesus, please help me learn to love everyone. Amen.

Theme: Christian Behavior

#114

God Wants You to Share His Love

Materials: *candle, matches, a large bowl, a darkened room*

"You should be a light for other people." Matthew 5:16.

In Bible times, most people lived in houses with only one room. At night their light came from a lamp made of a small dish of oil with a wick floating in it. It gave about as much light as this candle. *[Light the candle.]*

Jesus told a little story about these lamps. He said, "People don't hide a light under a bowl. They put the light on a lampstand. Then the light shines for all the people in the house" (Matthew 5:15).

Wouldn't it be silly to have a light and then cover it up? *[Cover the candle.]* The whole point of having a lamp is for it to give light. *[Uncover.]*

Jesus said, "You are a light. Don't hide it. Shine so others can see." What did He mean? Jesus wants us to be good examples.

How can we let our light shine? Our light shines in the way we treat our family. Our light shines in the way we love our neighbors. Our light shines when we are friendly, when we play fair, when we think about what others need.

We let our light shine by being good examples. We can be the light that helps others do the right thing. We can be the light that helps others find Jesus.

Dear Jesus, I'm going to let my light shine. Amen.

#115

Theme: Christian Behavior

It All Belongs to God

Materials: *play dough or supplies for homemade cookies; teapot or pitcher; cups and saucers; water; dolls or stuffed animals*

"The earth and everything in it belong to the Lord." Psalm 24:1.

Make cookies together or let your child make pretend cookies with play dough. Hold a tea party, inviting several dolls or stuffed animals. Let the child pour cups of water, while you pass around the real or pretend cookies. Ask each guest, "Would you like one of (your child's name)'s cookies?"]

It is fun to have a tea party, isn't it? What was your favorite part? Do you know what I liked best? I liked passing out the cookies. I asked everyone if they wanted one of your cookies.

Do you know why I said they were your cookies? Because you made them. If I were to call Grandma to tell her what we did today, I would probably say, "We had some of (child's name)'s cookies."

Even though you gave them away, I think of them as being your cookies—because you made them.

Who made our world? God did. He made the world and everything in it. And then He gave it to us to take care of.

It all belongs to Him. God made the oceans and deserts, the plants and animals, the rain and sunshine. Even though He gave it to us, this is God's world—because He made it.

Dear Jesus, thank You for making our world. Amen.

Theme: Stewardship

#116

Take Good Care of It

Materials: *crayons, a storybook, a coloring book*

"The Lord God put the man in the garden of Eden to care for it." Genesis 2:15.

L et's color together while we have our story. I have two books. Which book should we color in?

[Hold up the storybook.] This book is made for reading the story and looking at the pictures. We shouldn't color in this book.

[Hold up the coloring book.] This book is made for coloring in. These pictures will look even better after we use our crayons to add colors.

Choose a page in this coloring book. You color one side and I'll color the other. *[Color together while you continue the story.]*

It's important for you to learn to take good care of your things. How can you take good care of your storybook? *[Don't color in it, don't rip it, put it back on the bookshelf when you're done, etc. Discuss taking care of other possessions as interest permits.]*

When God made this world, He gave it to Adam and Eve. He told them to take good care of it.

God told them to take care of "every living thing" (Genesis 1:28). God wants us to take care of the animals and keep them safe. God wants us to take care of the plants and oceans and even the air. *[While you finish coloring, discuss ways you can take care of the environment.]*

Dear Jesus, I want to take good care of Your world. Amen.

#117

Theme: Stewardship

Send Me!

Materials: *treats to share, such as scented lip balm, gum, or strawberries*

"So I said, 'Here I am. Send me!'"
Isaiah 6:8.

ell your child to hide. Explain that when you need help, he / she is to come out and say, "Here I am. Send me!" Place the treat on the table. Go into another room and say, "I need [treat]. Who can I send?" Your child appears and says, "Here I am. Send me!" Explain that it's on the table. The child runs to get it, and you both enjoy it.]

One day, while Isaiah was at the Temple, he had a vision. He saw God! It was a most amazing sight. God was sitting on a high throne. There were heavenly creatures—maybe they were angels. They had six wings and they were so bright it looked as if they were burning. They were flying and calling to each other. Then everything began to shake, and the air was filled with smoke!

Isaiah was afraid; he felt as if he didn't deserve to see God. Then he heard God say, "Whom can I send?" And very bravely Isaiah answered, "Here I am. Send me!" Isaiah became God's helper.

You can work for God. When you see someone who needs help, God is asking you, "Whom can I send?" You can answer, "Here I am. Send me!" You can help.

Dear God, here I am. Send me! Amen.

Theme: Stewardship
LLFJ-18

#118

Helping

Materials: *an item of clothing that your child can put on without help, such as a sweater, hat or shoes; a doll or stuffed animal with an item of clothing that will fit it*

"The Son of Man did not come for other people to serve him. He came to serve others." Matthew 20:28.

When you were a baby, you didn't know how to dress yourself. I had to put your *[sweater]* on for you. But now you are so big, you can put your *[sweater]* on all by yourself, can't you? Show me how you can do it.

I'll bet you can even help someone else get dressed now. Let's pretend this *[stuffed bear]* needs help putting on his shirt. Can you help him?

That's what happens when you grow up. First you need help. Then you can help yourself. Then you can help others.

When Jesus was a baby, He needed help—as all babies do. But when He grew up, He spent His life helping others. He helped people who were sick. He helped people who were in trouble. He helped people who had questions. He told them how much God loved them.

Jesus showed us how we should live. He taught us that the way to be happy is by helping others.

As you get bigger, you can help more and more. You can spend your life helping others.

Dear Jesus, I want to be like You. I want to help others. Amen.

#119

Theme: Stewardship

Spend Your Time

Materials: *a quarter, some raisins, a ball, a clock or watch*

"Live wisely. I mean that you should use every chance you have for doing good." **Ephesians 5:15, 16.**

Here is a quarter. It is money. What are some things you could do with this quarter? *[Talk about options: spend, save, give away.]*

Here are some raisins. They are a treat. What are some things you could do with these raisins? *[Eat, save for later, share.]*

Here is a ball. It is a toy. What are some things you could do with this ball? *[Play with it, put it in your toy box, give it away.]*

When you have money, treats, and toys, you choose what to do with them. You can use them, save them, or give them away.

I am thinking of something else that we all have. Here is a hint: *[Show a clock or watch.]* Time. This clock helps us keep track of time. Time is a gift that God gives to all of us.

Time is different from other things. You can save your money, but you can't save your time. You can't put time in the bank or the cupboard or the toy box. You can only use it. Time is something you spend. We are spending it right now, together.

God is giving you the gift of time today. It is here for you to use. How will you spend it? You get to choose.

Dear Jesus, help me to spend my time wisely. Amen.

Theme: Stewardship

#120

God Wants You to Choose Him

Activity: *act out this story*

"Believe in the Lord Jesus and you will be saved." Acts 16:31.

Paul and his friend Silas were in jail. They were in trouble because they had been preaching about Jesus. They were praying and singing when all of a sudden there was an earthquake. The doors of the jail broke open.

The jailer saw that the doors were open, and he thought that all the prisoners had escaped. He knew he would be killed as punishment for letting them escape. But Paul shouted, "We're still here!"

The jailer ran inside. He was shaking with fear. He had heard Paul and Silas praying and singing. He could tell that they were happy. He wanted what they had. Right there in the middle of the disaster, he asked them how he could be saved. And they told him, "Believe."

Believe God loves you. Believe Jesus died for you. Believe God has a plan for your life—and you want to follow that plan.

The jailer believed, and his life was changed. He took Paul and Silas to his house. He fed them and washed their wounds. Paul and Silas taught the jailer and his family about Jesus—and they believed.

You can choose to believe. You can choose to follow God's plan for your life.

Dear God, I want to follow Your plan. Amen.

#121

Theme: Salvation

God Wants to Be With You

Materials: *a toy top or a wheel, play dough*

"I will take you to be with me so that you may be where I am." John 14:3.

Watch this. *[Spin the top or roll wheel.]* The top spins on a point, because everything on this top is balanced. It looks pretty spinning, doesn't it! What do you think would happen if I stuck some play dough on one side of the top? *[Or attach weight to the side of the wheel to put it out of balance.]* Let's spin the top and see what happens.

The top can't spin very well, can it? We messed it up when we put the play dough on it. It isn't balanced. Too much weight is on this side, and it makes the top wobble.

When the world was first created, everything was right. Everything was the way it should be. *[Take off the play dough so the top spins nicely.]*

Sin changed things. Sin put the world out of balance. *[Add the play dough and spin.]*

God wants to put the world right again. His plan is to make things perfect, like they were before sin. *[Take off the play dough.]* God wants to be with us. That's why Jesus is coming back to get us.

Someday Jesus will take us to heaven.

Dear Jesus, thank You for Your plan to take me to heaven. Amen.

Theme: Christ's Second Coming

#122

The Family of God

Materials: *two pieces of paper, stapler, crayons or markers, family photos*

"He loved us so much that we are called children of God." 1 John 3:1.

Make a booklet called "My Family." Fold papers in half and staple together. Fill the pages with drawings or photos of your family, as well as family facts such as: youngest / oldest person, address, phone number, birthdays, pets, favorite things to do together, ways you take care of each other, etc.]

I like this book. It tells about our family. Families take care of each other and do things together.

We belong to another family. It is a much bigger family—the family of God. God is our Father and we are His children. People who believe in Jesus are brothers and sisters.

In our family we take care of each other. [Look at that page in your booklet.] We take care of each other in the family of God too. We help our brothers and sisters who are in trouble. We comfort our brothers and sisters who are sad.

In our family we do things together. [Look at that page.] We do things together in the family of God, too. We meet together for church. We sing and pray together. We tell other people about Jesus—we want to make them a part of God's family too.

It is good to belong to the family of God.

Dear Jesus, thank You that I belong to the family of God. Amen.

#123

Theme: The Church

We Are His Hands

Materials: *two toy phones or real phones, or just hold your fist to your ear*

"All of you together are the body of Christ." 1 Corinthians 12:27.

Let's pretend I'm at the store and you're home. I'll call you on the phone. *[Pretend to dial. Ring. Child answers.]* "Hello. Could you look in the fridge and see if I need to buy milk?" *[Child checks.]* "OK, thanks for your help. I love you. 'Bye."

Want to do it again? *[Dial, ring, answer.]* "Hello. I think I forgot to turn off the lights in the basement. Can you make sure they are off? Thank you. 'Bye." *[Child checks to make sure lights are off.]*

That was fun. You are a good helper. I'm glad I can count on you when something needs to be done.

When Jesus was on earth, He helped people who were in trouble. He healed the sick and fed the hungry. He taught people about God.

But now Jesus is in heaven. He is counting on us to help Him. When someone is hungry or in trouble, Jesus depends on us to help. When people don't know the good news, Jesus needs us to tell them.

We are His hands. When we help others, our hands are doing what His did. We are His voice when we tell others about God. Since Jesus is not here, we are His body.

Dear Jesus, I will be Your hands. I will help others. Amen.

Theme: The Church

#124

Lots of Different Parts

Materials: *paper and pencil*

"A person's body has more than one part. It has many parts." 1 Corinthians 12:14.

I will describe a part of your body, and you point to it and say its name. Ready? You need these to hear. *[Child points to ears and says, "Ears."]* You bend these when you kneel. *[Knees.]* You use this to smell. *[Nose.] [Continue as long as it's fun.]*

You're good at this game. You know the parts of your body. You know the job that each part has.

Your body has many parts—ears, elbows, feet. They are all different, and they are all important. Your nose is important. You need it to smell. But it would be terrible if your face had only noses—and no eyes or mouth or ears. Can you draw a picture of what that would look like?

[Provide paper.] I think your picture clearly shows that a face needs all it parts.

In the Bible Paul says the church is like a body. A body has different parts—so does the church. What are the parts of the church? People! The church is made of people. They are all different. They have different jobs. And they are all important.

You wouldn't want a face with all noses. And you wouldn't want a church in which everyone was the same.

Dear Jesus, thank You for making different kinds of people. Amen.

#125

Theme: The Church

Working Together

Materials: *a piece of butcher paper or two sheets of newspaper taped together, marker or chalk, crayons or paint*

"There are many parts, but only one body." 1 Corinthians 12:20.

Have your child lie down on the paper; trace around his/her body with marker. Or do the same thing on the driveway using chalk. Let your child *add facial features, clothes, hair, etc.]*

Here is a life-size picture of you. It looks like you, but I can tell the difference. You are much wigglier. Let me see you wiggle your feet.

What you just did shows me how your body can work together. *[Point to body parts as you say them.]* Your ears heard me say, "Wiggle your feet." Your ears told your brain. Your brain told your feet to wiggle. Then your eyes looked at me and your mouth smiled. The different parts of your body worked together.

The parts didn't fight with each other. Your ears didn't say, "I'm not telling the brain what I heard, because I'm mad at it." Your left foot didn't say, "I won't wiggle, because the right foot always gets to go first." The parts get along. Each part does the work it is supposed to do.

That's how Jesus wants the church to be. There are many different people in the church. We need to work together. Each of us needs to do the work we are supposed to do.

Dear Jesus, help me learn to work with others. Amen.

Theme: The Church
LLFJ-19

Devotion

#126

Singing Together

Activity: *singing*

"Come, let's sing for joy to the Lord."
Psalm 95:1.

Do you like to sing? I love to hear you sing. One of the most important things we do when we go to church is sing. When we sing, we give praise to God—we say good things about the good things He has given us. When we sing praises, the words give praise and the music gives praise. It is twice as much praise. *[Sing a song of praise, such as "Praise Him, Praise Him.]*

In church we need different people to do different jobs when we sing. Someone needs to lead the singing. That person stands in front of everyone and tells us what song we're going to sing and helps us all start at the same time. It's nice to have people play the piano or organ or guitar. They help us all sing the same notes and go the same speed. And of course we need people to sing along—the more, the better.

Sometimes there is special music. Maybe only one or two people sing. Or maybe someone plays the trumpet or flute. The rest of us have an important job too—we listen!

We need each other when we sing in church. We sing together. We listen together. We praise God together.

Dear God, thank You that we can sing together. Amen.

#127

Theme: The Church

Praying Together

Materials: *Bible (King James Version)*

"Our Father which art in heaven, Hallowed be thy name." Matthew 6:9, KJV.

The disciples noticed that Jesus prayed a lot. They saw how peaceful He was after He prayed. They wanted to learn to pray like that. The disciples asked Jesus to teach them to pray.

So Jesus taught them a special prayer. We call it the Lord's Prayer because Jesus, our Lord, taught it to us. It is an example that can help us learn to pray.

The Lord's Prayer is a prayer that we can pray together. You can start to learn it. Most Christians know it by memory because we sometimes say it together in church.

It is here in the Bible. *[Turn to Matthew 6:9-13.]* While I read it, you listen to see if you've heard it before. *[Read it, then help your child memorize the first line.]*

Look at the first two words: Our Father. Jesus didn't teach us to say "My Father." He wants us to remember that God doesn't belong to only you or only me. In this entire prayer we never say "I" or "me."

This prayer reminds us that we are not alone. We belong to the family of God. God is our Father, and we have each other. When we get together, in church or anywhere, we can pray together.

Dear Jesus, thank You for teaching me to pray with the family of God. Amen.

Theme: The Church

#128

Giving Together

Materials: *a small box (like a shoe box); scissors; coins*

"People were happy to give their money."
2 Chronicles 24:10.

Joash was 7 years old when he became king. The first thing he did was get rid of the idols. Then he wanted to show the people how to worship the true God. They needed a place to worship.

There was a Temple, but it was a mess. It would cost a lot of money to fix it. Where would they get enough money? Joash made a plan.

He got a box and made a hole in the top of it. *[Make a hole in your box.]* He put the box by the gate. When the people came to the Temple, they put their offerings in the box.

The people were happy to give their money. They filled the box with money. *[Child puts money into the box.]* The priests took the money out and put the box back, and the people filled it up again and again. *[Act out.]*

The people wanted to help. They wanted to give their money. When the Temple was repaired, it was even stronger than before.

Together we can give to help our church. One person alone cannot give enough to take care of the buildings, electricity, papers, missionaries, and everything else. But if we all give, there can be plenty. We can give together.

Dear God, help me learn to do my part. Amen.

#129

Theme: The Church

Saying Thank You

Materials: *strips of paper to make a paper chain; pencil / crayons; tape / stapler*

"We give thanks to you, Lord God All-Powerful." Revelation 11:17.

I am thinking of two special words. You might even say they are magic words. Here is a hint. When you say these words, you show good manners. You say these words when someone gives you something or does something nice for you. You say thank you!

When you say thank you, it makes people happy. But saying thank you can make you happy too. Every time you say thank you it makes you a little less selfish and a little more grateful. Saying thank you is good for you.

Saying thank you is an important part of worship. We get together at church to say thank you to God. We thank Him for the things He has given us. We thank Him for the things He has done for us.

There are *[two]* of us together now. We can be thankful together. Let's make a thank-you chain. You tell me something you're thankful for, and I'll write it on this paper. *[Fasten it into a circle.]* Now I'll think of something I'm thankful for and write it on another paper. *[Link papers and fasten. Continue taking turns as long as it's fun.]*

Look at all these thank-yous linked together! We can say thank you together.

Dear God, thank You for [read the list from the thank-you chain]. *Amen.*

Theme: The Church

#130

Believing Together

Materials: *three bowls of water: one as hot as you can stand it, one cold with ice cubes, and one a very comfortable temperature*

"It is good and pleasant when God's people live together in peace!"
Psalm 133:1.

I have three bowls of water here. Let's put our hands in this bowl and feel the water. It's hot! Would you like to go swimming in this water? No! It's much too hot. Now let's try this bowl. It's cold! Would you like to take a bath in this water? No! It's much too cold. Now let's try this bowl. Ah! Doesn't that feel nice? We could play in this water all day.

Let's pretend that these bowls of water are churches. Which church would you like to go to? The one that's just right! The one that makes us feel comfortable and welcome.

Church is a place where you can go to be with people who believe the same things you believe. You can relax there. You don't have to worry that people will make fun of what you think. You can be comfortable at church because you know that the people love you and want you to be there. You can also help others be comfortable in church. *[Help your child think of things to do to help others be comfortable.]*

We go to church to worship together—to sing and pray and give and say thank you. We go to church to be together and help each other. We go to church to be with other people who love Jesus.

Dear Jesus, thank You for my church. Amen.

#131

Theme: The Church

God's Quilt

Materials: *a patchwork quilt or picture of a quilt; paper and crayons*

"Love is what holds you all together in perfect unity." Colossians 3:14.

We sing, pray, and give together. We work together. But we don't do the same work. We are all different. The church needs lots of different kinds of people. Some people are good leaders. They can make plans and organize things. Some people are good at sharing and helping others. Some people are good at making people feel welcome. Others are good at putting things in order and keeping things clean. Each of us is good at something.

[Show quilt.] This is a special kind of blanket. It's called a patchwork quilt. It is made of different colors and shapes sewn together. *[Your child can identify the different colors and shapes in the quilt.]* If this quilt were all one color, it might as well be a plain blanket—it is the different colors blending together that make it so beautiful.

God's church is like a quilt. It is made of different people who are good at different things. It is the different people working together that make it so beautiful. This quilt is sewn together with thread. What do you think holds together all the different people in the church? Love. God's love is the thread that holds us together.

[Draw a patchwork design on a paper and let your child color it.]

Dear God, thank You for making us all different. It's beautiful. Amen.

Theme: The Church

#132

Sweet Smells

Materials: *3 x 5 cards; white glue; pencil; spices and herbs, such as cloves, cinnamon, ginger, thyme, oregano*

"God uses us to spread his knowledge everywhere like a sweet-smelling perfume." 2 Corinthians 2:14.

Make a smell collection. Spread a little glue, perhaps in a heart shape, on a card. Sprinkle a little spice over the glue. Write the name of the spice at the bottom of the card. Make several cards.]

What a wonderful collection of smells we have. Which one is your favorite? I'm glad there are lots of different good smells.

Smells are kind of hard to understand, because we can't see them or feel them or hear them. We know they are there only because we can smell them.

We can't see or feel or hear the Holy Spirit, either. But we know He is here because He gives us gifts. Jesus sends us the Holy Spirit to help us.

The Holy Spirit gives us gifts so we can help one another. He helps us to be kind and thoughtful. He helps us learn to love and take care of one another.

The Holy Spirit gives us gifts so we can tell others about Jesus. The Holy Spirit helps us teach and preach. He shows us how our lights can shine.

There are many different gifts of the Spirit. All of them help us spread the Good News "everywhere like a sweet-smelling perfume."

Dear Jesus, thank You for sending the Holy Spirit to help me. Amen.

#133

Theme: Spiritual Gifts

Gifts for Everyone

Materials: *two dolls to act out the scenarios*

"We all have different gifts."
Romans 12:6.

The Holy Spirit gives different gifts to different people. Some people get the gift of prophecy. Samuel was a prophet. *[Use the dolls to act out Samuel delivering God's messages.]* Some people get the gift of faith. Noah needed a lot of faith. *[Doll builds the ark.]*

People in Bible times got gifts from the Holy Spirit. We get them today, too. The gifts of the Holy Spirit help us help others. The Holy Spirit helps some people to be good listeners. People who are in trouble can talk to these people, because they are patient and kind. *[Use dolls to act out.]*

Some people are good with people who are sick. They know how to make them feel more comfortable. They are sympathetic and gentle. *[Act out.]*

The gifts of the Holy Spirit help us tell others about Jesus. The Holy Spirit helps some people to be good teachers. They are able to help people understand ideas. They make it fun to learn. *[Act out.]* Some people are good preachers. They use words to help people want to know Jesus. They know how to tell good stories. *[Act out.]*

The Holy Spirit gives everybody a gift. He has a gift for you. What do you think it might be?

Dear God, thank You for all the gifts of the Holy Spirit. Amen.

Theme: Spiritual Gifts
LLFJ-20

#134

Gifts for You

Materials: *gift boxes, wrapping paper, tape. Prepare two or three "spiritual gifts" such as "cheerfulness," "helping," or "a good example." Pack small illustrations of each gift into each box. A smiley face sticker or picture of a smile for cheerfulness, a dish towel for helping, etc. Wrap the boxes with gift wrap.*

"The Spirit decides what to give each person." 1 Corinthians 12:11.

Here are some gifts. I got them ready, but let's pretend they are from the Holy Spirit. The Bible says the Holy Spirit gives us gifts. Would you like to open these gifts and see what He may have given you?

[Let your child open the gifts one at a time. Talk about what each gift means. Following are examples of what you might say.]

There's a smile in this box! The Holy Spirit can give you the gift of cheerfulness. You are cheerful. You make the people around you feel cheerful. When I see your smile, it makes me happy. Can you think of a way your cheerfulness could help someone?

There is a dish towel in this box. What do you do with a dish towel? You can help do the dishes! Being helpful is a gift from the Holy Spirit. People who are good at being helpful do things that need to be done. They love helping! The gifts of the Spirit make us happy when we use them.

The Holy Spirit has wonderful gifts for you.

Dear Jesus, thank You for giving me such wonderful gifts. Amen.

#135

Theme: Spiritual Gifts

Use Your Gifts

Materials: *three dolls, 15 coins; line the dolls up and let your child hand out the coins as you tell the story*

"Be good servants and use your gifts to serve each other." 1 Peter 4:10.

Jesus told a story about three servants. A man was going on a trip. He called his three servants. He gave one servant five coins. He gave another servant two coins. He gave the last servant one coin. Then he left.

The servant with five coins used that money to make more money. He earned five more coins. The servant with two coins used the money to make more money. He earned two more coins. But the servant with one coin dug a hole and buried his coin.

When the master came home he asked his servants what they'd done with the money. The first servant showed him his five coins and the five coins he had earned. The master said, "You did well." The second servant showed him his two coins and two more coins. The master said, "You did well." But the third servant said, "I hid your coin in a hole. Here it is."

The master was upset. He hadn't given him a coin because he wanted him to hide it. He had wanted him to use it.

Why did Jesus tell this story? He wants us to use our gifts from the Holy Spirit—not hide them.

Use your gifts. They are yours to enjoy.

Dear Jesus, thank You for my gifts. Help me to use them. Amen

Theme: Spiritual Gifts

#136

Name That Tree

Materials: *crayons. Draw a picture of a tree on three or four lunch-sized bags. Place a different type of fruit in each bag [apple, orange, banana, etc.].*

"Each tree is known by its fruit."
Luke 6:44.

Let's play "Name That Tree." Each of these bags has a piece of fruit in it. Reach into the bag and feel the fruit. What kind of fruit do you think it is? Take it out and see. It's an apple! *[Write "apple tree" on the bag. Let child draw apples on the tree. Repeat with remaining bags.]*

[Point to apple tree bag.] How did we know this was an apple tree? We saw the apple. When we see the fruit we are able to figure out the name of the tree. Apples grow on apple trees.

Once when Jesus was teaching He said, "Each tree is known by its fruit." Do you think He was talking about trees and fruit only? No.

He wanted us to think about how people are like trees and fruit.

Pretend you are a tree. I should be able to tell what kind of tree you are by looking at your fruit. But what kind of fruit does a little boy/girl have?

I know! I will look at the things you do. Let's see. You have a happy smile on your face. You must be a happy tree! You are listening carefully to what I am saying. You must be an obedient tree!

I can tell what kind of a person you are by looking at the things you do.

Dear Jesus, help me to have good fruit. Amen.

#137

Theme: Christian Behavior

Fruits of the Spirit

Materials: *a big piece of paper; crayons or markers*

"Live by following the Spirit."
Galatians 5:16.

P aul was a missionary. He went from city to city telling the good news. One day he heard that his friends in Galatia were having trouble. Some new teachers had come to town, and they were teaching wrong ideas. These new teachers were saying that a person needed to keep all the laws in order to be saved. Now, what's wrong with that? It's good to obey the law, isn't it? Of course!

But these teachers said: You can save yourself if you keep the law. That's wrong! We can't save ourselves. Only Jesus can save us from sin. We need Jesus.

So Paul wrote a letter to his friends. He told them that they could not save themselves by following the law. Jesus saves us. Paul wanted to be sure they knew that the Holy Spirit would help them do the right thing.

In his letter Paul uses that idea about people being like fruit trees. Paul says that the Holy Spirit will help you grow wonderful fruit—fruits of the Spirit!

We will talk about this fruit for the next few days. Let's make a paper tree. We'll pretend that this tree is you, and each day we'll add a fruit of the Spirit.

Dear Jesus, thank You for the fruits of the Spirit. Amen.

Theme: Christian Behavior

#138

Love

Materials: *a bell, cymbal, or other percussion instrument; a heart-shaped paper with LOVE written on it*

"The greatest of these is love."
1 Corinthians 13:13.

Paul says that the Holy Spirit will help you grow wonderful fruit. Do you know what the first fruit is? Love. Paul wants us to know that love is the most important thing.

Paul wrote another letter to some friends who were arguing about the gifts of the Spirit. They were arguing about which gift was most important.

Paul told them, "The gifts don't matter if you don't have love."

Some people were saying that the gift of prophecy was most important. Paul wrote, "Maybe you know all of God's secrets. But if you don't have love, they won't mean anything."

Some people were saying that the gift of speaking was most important. Paul said, "Maybe you can speak as beautifully as an angel. But if you don't have love, your words are just noise. You are just a noisy bell or a ringing cymbal."

I am going to try to give you a message with this bell. *[Ring the bell a few times.]* Could you understand my message? No. It's just noise. It doesn't mean anything.

Love gives everything meaning. Love is the first fruit of the Holy Spirit. It's the sweetest fruit of all. *[Stick the paper heart on the tree you made in the previous lesson.]*

Dear Jesus, help me learn to love. Amen.

#139

Theme: Christian Behavior

Joy

Materials: *paper, pencil, eraser, marker; a heart-shaped paper with JOY on it*

"Be full of joy in the Lord always. I will say again, be full of joy." Philippians 4:4.

L et's think of some things that make you happy. How about cookies? *[Write "cookies" with pencil. Think of other trivial things, such as toys or entertainment.]*

Now, do you think it is possible to be happy without cookies? I would be sad for a while if I couldn't have cookies anymore. But I could learn to be happy without them. *[Erase "cookies." Talk about other items on the list, then erase them.]*

Happiness doesn't depend on things. We can have happy lives without these things.

Paul says the Holy Spirit will help us grow fruit. Joy is one of those fruits. The Holy Spirit can make us joyful.

Paul wrote a letter about joy to his friends in Philippi. Poor old Paul was in jail. He was cold and lonely and in big trouble because he'd been preaching about Jesus. But Paul was happy. Do you know why? Paul had Jesus. *[Write "Jesus" with marker.]* No one could take that away. *[Demonstrate that it won't erase.]* Jesus brings us real joy.

On Paul's list of fruits of the Spirit, joy is second on the list, right after love. When there is love, joy will follow. *[Add JOY heart to the tree.]*

Dear Jesus, help me learn to be joyful. Amen.

Theme: Christian Behavior

#140

Peace

Materials: *paper heart with PEACE on it. Let child help provide special effects with electric fan, squirt bottle, pot lids, flashlight*

"The peace that God gives is so great that we cannot understand it." Philippians 4:7.

Make the room dark.] Jesus had been teaching all day. He said to His disciples, "Come with me across the lake" (Mark 4:35). So they got into a boat and began to sail. *[Climb onto couch or bed.]* Jesus was tired. He fell asleep.

Then a very strong wind began to blow. *[Turn on the fan.]* It was raining hard, and the waves were splashing into the boat. *[Squirt some water into the air.]* It was a terrible storm, with thunder and lightning. *[Crash lids and turn flashlight on and off.]*

Jesus was sound asleep. The disciples were scared. They thought the boat would sink. They yelled, "Teacher, we will drown!"

Jesus stood up. He spoke to the wind: "Quiet!" He told the waves, "Be still!" The storm went away. Everything was peaceful.

Paul says we can have fruits of the Spirit. The third fruit is peace. The Holy Spirit can bring you the peace of Jesus. *[Add PEACE heart to the tree.]*

Sometimes when we have troubles, we say they are like a storm. We can ask Jesus to be with us in the storm. He doesn't always tell the storm to go away. But He will be with us. He will give us peace.

Dear Jesus, help me not to be worried. I want Your peace. Amen.

#141

Theme: Christian Behavior

Patience

Materials: *paper heart with PATIENCE on it; paper plate, scissors, yarn, glue, markers*

"God's holy people must be patient." Revelation 14:12.

L ion cubs love to play. A mother lion is very patient. She lets her cubs pounce on her. She swishes her tail so the cubs can try to catch it. She lets them growl at her. *[Act this out as you lie on the floor while the children play around and on you. Pretend your hand and arm is a tail.]* Sometimes the cubs play too rough and the lioness has to teach them respect. But usually she is patient with her babies.

Why does the mother lion put up with this? She could easily smack them with her paw. But she lets them play because she knows it is important. When they jump and wrestle they are learning how to become good hunters. The mother lion is patient while her babies learn.

Paul says that patience is one of the fruits of the Spirit. The Holy Spirit can help you be patient. *[Add PATIENCE heart to the tree.]*

Are there some people who drive you crazy? They won't share, they whine, they tattle. When you are around people like that you might want to smack them. But that wouldn't be a good idea. If you hit them, they'll want to hit you back, and then things will just get worse.

It's better to be patient. The Holy Spirit will help you. *[Make lion masks with the paper plates. Then have a little tussle.]*

Dear Jesus, help me learn to be patient. Amen.

Theme: Christian Behavior

#142

Kindness

Materials: *paper heart with KINDNESS on it*

"Be kind and loving to each other."
Ephesians 4:32.

Review the fruits on the "Fruits of the Spirit" tree you've been making.] Now let's add kindness to the tree. Paul says the Holy Spirit will help us be kind. [Add KINDNESS heart.]

When Paul wrote his list of fruits of the Spirit, he had been having lots of trouble. He had been in jail. People had thrown stones at him. People had chased him and yelled at him. Most of the time people weren't kind to Paul. They were mean because he preached about Jesus. It doesn't look as if Paul had much of the "kindness" fruit of the Spirit.

But he did. The kindness fruit isn't "other people being kind to you." The kindness fruit is

"you being kind to other people."

Paul knew that he could choose to be kind. If people were mean to him, he didn't have to be mean back. He could choose to be kind. The Holy Spirit gave him the fruit of kindness.

The Holy Spirit will help us choose to be kind. Many times every day we get to decide if we will be kind or not. We can choose to be kind to our family, friends, and animals. Let's think of a way to be kind right now.

Dear Jesus, help me always choose to be kind. Amen.

Theme: Christian Behavior

Goodness

Materials: *paper heart with GOODNESS on it; a print or painting of Jesus; one of your child's drawings (perhaps you could have him/her draw a picture of Jesus)*

**"I am sure that you are full of goodness."
Romans 15:14.**

Next on Paul's list of fruits of the Spirit is goodness. The Holy Spirit can help us to be good. *[Add GOODNESS heart to the tree.]*

[Show the famous painting.] Look at this picture. It was painted by a famous artist. *[Discuss why you like the painting—the beautiful colors, the way it almost looks real, the expression on Jesus' face, etc.]* This is a good picture. You can look at famous pictures like this and admire them and learn from them.

[Show child's drawing.] Look at this picture. You made it. *[Discuss why you like it. Point out what you like best, how it makes you feel, etc.]*

This is a good picture too.

These pictures are not the same, but they are both good. They are what they should be.

Jesus said, "Only God is good (Matt. 19:17). We cannot be good the way God is good. *[Point to famous painting.]*

But we can be good the way people should be. We can learn about God's goodness. The more we know God, the more we will want to be like Him. The more we know God, the more His goodness will show in our lives. The Holy Spirit will help us to be good.

Dear Jesus, help me to be good. I want to know you better. Amen.

Theme: Christian Behavior

#144

Faithfulness

Materials: *paper heart with FAITHFULNESS on it*

"The Lord is faithful. He will give you strength." 2 Thessalonians 3:3.

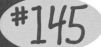

Let's see how many things you can do at the same time. First, stand up. Good. Now smile. Keep standing and smiling. Now put your arms out like an airplane. Leave them out and wiggle your fingers. Nod your head. Now lift one foot. OK, you're standing, smiling, your arms are out, your fingers are wiggling, you're nodding your head, and you're standing on one foot. Great! Now, do that all day. What? Nobody could do that all day! You can stop. But I'll tell you something you can do all the time. You do it even when you're sleeping! Can you guess? You breathe! In and out, all day and all night. Is it hard to do? Of course not.

Look at our "Fruits of the Spirit" tree. It shows how Christians should behave. *[Read each paper heart.]* The next fruit of the Spirit is faithfulness. When we are faithful, people can count on us to do these things all the time. Just like breathing! When we don't have God's Spirit, trying to do what is right all the time is like trying to stand on one foot, smile, wiggle, and nod all at once, all the time. We can't! But the Holy Spirit can help us be faithful.

Every morning we give ourselves to God, and His Spirit keeps us faithful. *[Add FAITHFULNESS heart to tree.]*

Dear Jesus, help me to be faithful. Amen.

#145

Theme: Christian Behavior

Gentleness

Materials: *bubbles and bubble wands; paper heart with GENTLENESS on it*

"Learn from me. I am gentle and humble in spirit." Matthew 11:29.

et's blow bubbles. It's not as easy as it looks. You have to blow just right—not too soft, not too hard. If you blow too soft, the bubbles won't form. *[Demonstrate.]* If you blow too hard, the bubble splatters all over. *[Demonstrate.]* It takes practice to learn exactly how to blow. You need to blow gently. *[Let child practice.]*

The word "gentle" can be confusing. Some people think it means the same thing as "weak." But it doesn't. Being gentle means being exactly as strong as you need to be. When you blow bubbles, you need to be gentle—not too soft, not too hard. When you play tug-of-war

with a puppy, you need to pull gently—not too weak, not too strong.

Jesus was gentle. He always knew exactly how strong to be. Not too strong—children were never afraid of Him. Not too weak—even a storm obeyed Him.

Gentleness is the next fruit in Paul's list of fruits of the Spirit. The Holy Spirit can help you be gentle. You can speak gently. You can play gently. You can be as strong as you need to be. *[Add GENTLENESS to tree.]*

Dear Jesus, help me be gentle. Amen.

Theme: Christian Behavior

#146

Self-control

Materials: *photo of your child, popsicle stick, glue; paper and pencil; paper heart with SELF-CONTROL on it*

"Get wisdom, self-control and understanding." Proverbs 23:23.

M*ake a puppet—cut out a photo of your child and glue it to the top of a popsicle stick.]*

We have come to the end of Paul's list of fruits of the Spirit. There is one more fruit to talk about—self-control. The Holy Spirit will help you be in control of what you do and say. A person with no self-control does the wrong thing and says, "I couldn't help it." A person who has self-control makes good choices.

Look at all these wonderful fruits *[point]:* love, joy, peace, patience, kindness, goodness, faithfulness, gentleness. *[Add "self-control" fruit.]* We can't do these things without help from the Holy Spirit, can we? We need to give Jesus control of our lives.

Now here's a tricky question. If Jesus is in control, why do we need self-control? Here's why: we are not puppets. Look at this little puppet. We are in control of it. We can talk for it. We can make it jump around. This puppet has no control.

We have control of ourselves. When we choose to follow Jesus, we still must make choices and decisions. When we give control to Jesus, we ask Him to help us. When we give Jesus control, He gives us self-control.

Dear God, I give you control of my life. Please give me self-control. Amen.

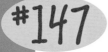

#147

Theme: Christian Behavior

I Will Come Back

Materials: *three dolls (or action figures, stuffed animals, paper dolls, etc.) to represent your child, yourself, and a baby-sitter*

"I will come back to you." John 14:18.

Sometimes I have to go out and I can't take you along. *[Use the dolls to act out what you say.]* I can't leave you alone—that wouldn't be safe. So I leave you with a baby-sitter.

While I am gone I might work or go shopping or have dinner. I have a nice time, but I miss you.

While you are with the baby-sitter you might play or have a snack or take a nap. You have fun with your baby-sitter, but you miss me.

After I am done with my work or my shopping, do you know what I do? I come back and get you. I always come back. *[Your dolls wave goodbye to the baby-sitter doll.]*

Jesus is in heaven. He loves us very much. He misses us. He wants to be with us.

Before Jesus left this earth to go to heaven, He promised that He would come back and get us. He promised He would take us to heaven. He promised that someday we would be with Him. Jesus will come back.

Because we love Jesus, this is our hope. We are waiting for Jesus to come get us, and we hope it will be soon. We want to be with Jesus.

Dear Jesus, I want to be with You, too. Amen.

Theme: Christ's Second Coming

#148

Picture Perfect

Materials: *a jigsaw puzzle of suitable difficulty for your child—one with a nature scene would be nice*

"Through Christ, God decided to bring all things back to himself again."
Colossians 1:20.

Let's do a puzzle together. Before we dump the pieces out, take a good look at the picture so you know what it's supposed to look like. *[As you work together, share secrets of successful puzzling (e.g., turn the pieces rightside up, do the corners and edges first, use color clues and shape clues). When you've finished, admire the puzzle together.]*

When God created the world it was perfect. *[Run your hand over the puzzle.]* Then sin came along and ruined the perfect picture. *[Break up the puzzle.]* But God had a plan to put the picture back together. *[Begin putting the puzzle together.]* He promised to send a Redeemer to rescue people from sin.

Jesus was our Redeemer. When He died on the cross He took the punishment for our sin. *[Keep working on the puzzle.]*

The next step in the plan is for Jesus to take us home to heaven. In heaven there will not be any sin. God will make everything new. Things will be perfect, like they were when the world was first created.

When we are in heaven, God's plan will be complete. *[Finish up the puzzle.]* God will put all the pieces back together. He will make the picture perfect again.

Dear Jesus, thank You for Your promise of heaven. Amen.

#149

Theme: Christ's Second Coming

Why Jesus Went Away

Materials: *Plan visit from a friend. (If you can't actually have a friend over, plan what you would do if you could.)*

"I am going there to prepare a place for you." John 14:2.

Here is some good news! *[A friend]* is going to come over to visit. You can play together and have fun. We'd better get ready. Maybe we should clean up your room. What toys do you think you'll want to play with? Do you think we should have a snack? *[Continue making plans and preparations.]* It's fun to have a friend over. Part of the fun is getting ready. We can look forward to having fun together.

Jesus is getting ready for us to come live with Him. When Jesus ate His last supper with the disciples, he told them, "I will be with you only a little longer" (John 13:33). The disciples were sad. Jesus was their best friend. What would they do without Him? Jesus said, "Don't worry. Trust Me." He gave them some good news: "I will come back" (John 14:3).

Then He gave them the best news of all. Jesus told them where He was going and why He was coming back: He was going to heaven to get things ready for all the people who choose to live with Him. He's coming back to take us there so we can be together.

Jesus is in heaven right now, getting things ready for us.

Dear Jesus, I'm looking forward to being in heaven with You. Amen.

Theme: Christ's Second Coming

LLFJ-22

#150

Jesus Is Bringing Us to God

Materials: *blue fabric or garment; pillows; small doll or action figure; things to build a bridge (e.g., boards, books, toys); Post-it Notes to make signs; pencil*

"We can enter through a new way that Jesus opened for us." Hebrews 10:20.

Let's make a river. *[Lay down the blue fabric.]* Now let's make high banks on the river. *[Lay pillows along the edges of the river.]* Pretend this is you. *[Show the doll.]* You want to get to the other side of the river. What would be the best way to get across? *[Discuss. Decide that a bridge would be best. Build a bridge out of something.]*

Now you can cross the river, because there is a bridge.

This bridge reminds me of Jesus. Let's pretend that this side of the river is our world. *[Make a sign that says WORLD for this side.]* You are here. God is over there on the other side, in heaven. *[Make HEAVEN sign.]* God would like to be with you, and you would like to be with God. The river will be sin. *[Make SIN sign and place it on the river.]* Sin keeps us away from God.

How will you get across? Who will be the bridge?

Jesus is the bridge. *[Make JESUS sign for the bridge.]*

When Jesus came to earth, He brought God to us. He showed us what God is like. Now Jesus is in heaven. He is bringing us to God.

Dear Jesus, thank You for bringing me to God. Amen.

#151

Theme: The Heavenly Sanctuary

God Is Fair

Materials: *three popsicle sticks; felt-tip pen; Post-it Note for a skirt; yarn for hair*

"The nations should be glad and sing because you judge people fairly." Psalm 67:4.

Make three figures out of popsicle sticks—one with a happy face, one with a mean face, and another happy one with a skirt or hair.] Let's tell a story with these puppets. Their names are Smiley, Grumpy, and Teacher.

Smiley was playing with his toy. Grumpy came over and took it away. Smiley said, "I want my toy back." Grumpy said, "No. It's mine."

Smiley went to tell Teacher, "Grumpy took my toy and won't give it back." Teacher went over to Grumpy. Grumpy said, "No. It's mine." Teacher knew the toy belonged to Smiley. She took the toy away from Grumpy and gave it back to Smiley.

Did Teacher do the right thing? Yes. Teacher was fair. We like things to be fair.

God is fair. God always does the right thing.

God is fair. He lets everyone choose. You can choose if you want to follow God's plan. You can decide if you want to believe that Jesus saved you from sin.

We get to decide. And someday God will decide. God will decide who has chosen to follow Him. God is fair. He knows who wants to be with Him, and who doesn't. He will always do the right thing.

Dear God, I praise You because You are fair. Amen.

Theme: The Heavenly Sanctuary

#152

If You're With Jesus

Activity: *a pretend parade*

"He went into heaven itself. He is there now before God to help us." Hebrews 9:24.

Let's pretend we're going to a parade. What kinds of things will we see? Now let's pretend that we get to the parade and there are lots of people already there, standing in front of us. I can see OK because I am tall. But you can't see the parade because you are short. All you can see are people's legs.

What can we do? I can pick you up or put you on my shoulders. Now you can see. *[Pick child up.]* It doesn't matter that you're not tall. You are with me. I can pick you up.

You may be worried that you won't be able to go to heaven because you make mistakes. You may be worried that you aren't good enough. You don't need to worry about that.

Everyone makes mistakes. No one is good enough. We can't get into heaven by being good. That's not how it works.

We get into heaven because of Jesus. Jesus is good. If we are with Jesus, He will take us in with Him.

It doesn't matter if you're not tall. You can see the parade if you're with me. It doesn't matter if you're not perfect. You can go to heaven if you're with Jesus.

Dear Jesus, I want to be with You. Amen.

#153

Theme: The Heavenly Sanctuary

Don't Just Stand There

Materials: *two wooden spoons, crayons, two white napkins or paper towels, two wire twisters (like you use to close plastic bags of produce at the grocery store)*

"Why are you standing here looking into the sky? Acts 1:11.

Just before Jesus went back to heaven, He reminded His disciples that they wouldn't be alone. The Holy Spirit would be with them and would give them the power they needed to tell other people the good news about Jesus. They would have the power to obey Jesus' command to love one another. Jesus told them that while they waited for Him to come back they had work to do. Then Jesus started to rise up into the air. The disciples tipped their heads back and watched Him go higher and higher until He disappeared into the clouds. The disciples stood there, staring into the sky, hoping to catch one last glimpse of Jesus.

Suddenly two angels wearing white clothes appeared. *[You make one angel and your child makes the other. With crayons, draw faces on the bowls of the spoons. Fasten the napkin around the "necks" with the twister. Use these angels to act out the rest of the story.]* The angels said, "Why are you standing here looking into the sky?" The angels reminded the disciples that they needed to stop standing around. They had work to do. "He will come back," the angels said (Acts 1:11). So the disciples went off to get ready.

Dear Jesus, help me remember to share Your love. Amen.

Theme: Christ's Second Coming

#154

Waiting

Materials: *a large bag containing items typically found in a pediatrician's waiting room (e.g., magazines, books, crayons, small toys)*

"We should live like that while we are waiting for the coming of our great God and Savior Jesus Christ." Titus 2:13.

When we go to the doctor, there is a room where we wait until the doctor is ready to see us. It's called the waiting room. There are usually some things in the waiting room so people will have something to do while they wait. I have some things like that in this bag. Can you guess what kinds of things are in a waiting room?

[Let the child guess and/or reach into the bag to feel the samples, then pull them out and look at them.]

We spend a lot of time waiting. We have to wait in line at the grocery store. We have to wait for our food at a restaurant. We have to wait for our turn on the swings. It's nice if we can have something to do while we wait.

Jesus knows that we are waiting for Him to come take us to heaven. But He doesn't want us just to stand around and wait. He wants us to have something to do while we wait.

Jesus wants us to be kind to each other and help each other while we wait. We can tell other people about God. We can learn more about Jesus every day so we can learn to be friends with Him.

When we do these things, we are getting ready for Jesus to come.

Dear Jesus, I want to be ready when You come again. Amen.

#155

Theme: Christ's Second Coming

It's a Surprise!

Materials: *a minute timer (you can use the one on your oven or microwave)*

"But the day the Lord comes again will be a surprise." 2 Peter 3:10.

Look at this! It's a minute timer. We can use it to tell us when a certain amount of time is up. Watch how it works. I'll set it for 20 seconds, and we'll watch the numbers count down. The numbers show how many seconds are left; when it gets to zero the buzzer tells us that the time is up.

After I set the timer I can see how much time is left before the buzzer rings. It is easy to know exactly when it will ring.

Sometimes we know exactly when things are going to happen. We know when your birthday is coming. We know what time Sabbath school starts. We know when the minute timer will ring.

There are other things that we know will happen, but we don't know exactly when they are going to happen. We knew that you were going to be born, but we weren't sure exactly what day. We know the letter carrier will bring our mail, but we don't know exactly what time. And we know that Jesus will come, but we don't know exactly when.

Jesus didn't say **when** He would come. But He said that He **would** come. Someday—maybe soon—Jesus will come take us to heaven.

Dear Jesus, I am waiting for You to take me to heaven. Amen.

Theme: Christ's Second Coming

#156

What Would You Do?

Activity: *Discuss responses to different situations*

"So always be ready. You don't know the day your Lord will come."
Matthew 24:42.

Let's play "What would you do?" I'll tell you two stories, and you tell me what you'd do if that happened.

Here's the first story. I want you to pick up your toys, so I say, "I want all these toys put away by Christmas *[or birthday or other event a long time away]*." What would you do? *[Discuss —that's a lot of time; there would be no hurry; the job would be put off and most likely forgotten.]*

Here's another story. I don't want your room to be a mess. So I tell you that when you're finished playing with a toy, you need to put it back where it belongs. What would you do? *[Discuss—child would learn good habit, room would be neat.]*

Jesus did not say when He was coming back. What if Jesus had said, "I will come back in 2,000 years"? Would the disciples have worked hard to tell everyone the good news? Probably not. They would have felt there was no hurry.

We have a job to do while we wait for Jesus. Jesus doesn't want us to put it off. He doesn't want us to forget about it. So He didn't tell us when He would come back. He wants us always to be ready.

Dear Jesus, Help me always to remember that You are coming. Amen.

#157

Theme: Christ's Second Coming

Be Ready

Materials: *a marker. Prepare by drawing two eyes and a smile on the fingertips of your right hand and sad faces on the left-hand fingertips.*

"Be ready! Be dressed for service and have your lamps shining." Luke 12:35.

Jesus told a story about being ready. Once there were 10 girls. *[Hold up your fingers.]* Five of them were wise. *[Draw smiley faces on your child's right fingertips.]* Five of them were foolish. *[Draw sad faces on left fingertips.]* The girls were invited to a wedding.

The wedding was at night, so the girls needed to bring a light. The five wise girls knew that weddings seldom start on time, so they brought extra oil for their lamps. The five foolish girls didn't think about bringing extra oil.

And sure enough, the groom was late. He was so late that the girls got sleepy and took a nap. *[Fingers take a nap.]* Their lamps went out.

Then someone called, "The groom is coming!" *[Fingers wake up.]* The wise girls poured their extra oil into their lamps and went to the wedding party. The foolish girls didn't have oil. They went to get some, but by the time they got back, the door was closed and they couldn't get into the party.

Why were these five girls wise? They were ready. Even though the groom didn't come when they thought he would, they were ready when he finally did come.

Jesus wants us to be ready. He will come.

Dear Jesus, I want to be wise. I want to be ready. Amen.

Theme: Christ's Second Coming

#158

Don't Be Afraid

Materials: *paper and crayons*

"Don't be afraid. These things must happen before the end comes."
Matthew 24:6.

Let's draw pictures of things we are afraid of. *[Draw a spider or something else.]* Here is a spider. It startles me when I see a spider. I'm afraid it will crawl on me. Now it's your turn. *[Take turns drawing and talking about two or three fearsome objects.]* Sometimes when we talk about things we're afraid of, they don't seem so scary.

When Jesus was here on earth, His followers wanted to know what the end of the world would be like. Jesus said it's going to be scary. There will be wars and riots. There will be earthquakes and sickness. In some places people won't have enough to eat, and in other places people will be mean to anyone who loves Jesus.

Jesus told His followers it would not be easy for them. But then Jesus said something very important: "Don't be afraid." We don't need to be afraid, because Jesus will take care of us. We don't need to worry, because God has a plan.

Scary things are happening all around us. But Jesus tells us, "None of these things can really harm you" (Luke 21:18). Jesus is with us. He will make sure everything turns out all right.

In the end, Jesus will win—and we are on His side.

Dear Jesus, thank You for taking care of me. Amen.

#159

Theme: Christ's Second Coming

What Will the Future Be Like?

Materials: *costumes and props to represent several career options*

"Now I have warned you about this before it happens." Matthew 24:25.

Has anyone ever said this to you: "What do you want to be when you grow up?" I have some costumes here. Try them on and see how you like them. *[Try on the different "careers."]*

Which did you like best? It's fun to try on costumes and think about what you might be. We like to wonder what the future will be like.

Jesus' disciples asked Him about the future. He told them some things to watch for. He said there would be wars and earthquakes and other troubles. He also said that people might try to trick us.

Someone might say, "I heard that Jesus is in the desert!" Don't believe it. Someone might come up to you and say, "I am Jesus. I've come back to earth." It won't be true.

Jesus said He won't come back that way. When He comes back everyone will see Him.

Jesus gave us some hints about our future. He told us what it will be like when He comes again so we won't be tricked.

Even more important, we need to become good friends with Jesus. The better we know Jesus, the less likely someone will be able to fool us this way.

Dear Jesus, I want to know You well so I won't be fooled. Amen.

Theme: Christ's Second Coming

#160

Here's a Hint

Materials: *paper and pencil*

"The Good News about God's kingdom will be preached in all the world." Matthew 24:14.

I'm thinking of a person. I'll give you some hints and you try to guess who it is *[e.g., she wears glasses, we talk to her on the phone, she has a cat]*. That's right! It's Grandma. *[Play a few more rounds.]*

Would you like to know when Jesus will come again? Jesus didn't tell us exactly, but he gave us one really big hint.

Here it is: "The Good News about God's kingdom will be preached in all the world, to every nation. Then the end will come" (Matthew 24:14).

God wants everyone everywhere to hear the good news. *[Draw an ear at the top of the page.]* God wants everyone everywhere to know that He loves them. *[Draw a heart in the middle.]* God wants everyone everywhere to have a chance to choose Him. *[Draw a smiley face and a grumpy face at the bottom.]*

How will everyone everywhere hear the good news? *[Point to ear.]* We can tell them. How will everyone everywhere know that God loves them? *[Point to heart.]* We can show them by the way we love them. How will everyone everywhere get a chance to choose God? *[Point to faces.]* We can give them that chance. Then Jesus will come.

Dear God, help me to show Your love to everyone. Amen.

Theme: Christ's Second Coming

Time Is Different for God

Materials: *Bible, clock with a second hand, puzzle*

"He does not want anyone to be lost."
2 Peter 3:9.

Jesus didn't come back as soon as Peter had hoped, but Peter never gave up hope. Peter wrote a letter to his friends explaining why Jesus hadn't come back yet. Here is what Peter wrote: *[Read 2 Peter 3:8, 9.]*

Peter says time is not the same for God as it is for people. What does he mean? *[Watch the second hand.]* You can see that time always moves the same, but time can seem to be slow or fast. I'll show you. Try to hold your breath for 30 seconds. *[Time yourself on the clock.]* Whew! That 30 seconds seemed like a very long time. Now you can try to do this puzzle in 30 seconds. *[Time it.]* Hey! That seemed like a very short time.

Time seems to move slow or fast depending on what you are doing. We might think that Jesus is taking a very long time to come back, because we want Him to come more than anything.

God wants to come too, but there is something He wants even more. Peter tells us in his letter: More than anything else, God wants to save us. That is more important to Him than coming back quickly.

"We are saved because our Lord is patient" (verse 15).

Dear Jesus, thank You for being patient with me. Amen.

Theme: Christ's Second Coming

#162

They Won't Miss Out

Activity: *Bible*

"Those who have died and were in Christ will rise first." 1 Thessalonians 4:16.

Let's pretend we're going to go swimming—but first, you have to take a nap. I say, "Take a nap, and at 3:00 we'll go swimming." OK, lie down and pretend to take a nap.

Now let's pretend it's 3:00 and you are still asleep. What should I do? Should I say, "He's still sleeping, so I guess we won't go"? Or should I wake you up and say, "Time to go swimming"?

I think I should wake you up. You wouldn't want to miss out on something fun because you were sleeping.

The Christians who lived in Thessalonica were worried. They expected Jesus to come soon, and they knew it was going to be wonderful. But they were worried that their friends who had already died would miss out on something special when Jesus came back. So Paul wrote them a letter. Here it is in the Bible. *[Open Bible to 1 Thessalonians 4.]* Paul tells the Christians in Thessalonica not to worry. Their friends won't miss anything. They will get to see Jesus when He comes.

When Jesus comes He will "wake up" the dead people who believed in Him. Everyone who loves Jesus gets to see Him coming to take them to heaven.

Dear Jesus, I'm glad that everyone will get to see You when You come. Amen.

Theme: Death and Resurrection

God Gives Life

Materials: *a candle, matches*

"A time is coming when all who are dead and in their graves will hear his voice." John 5:28.

[T]alk about the death of an acquaintance or a person in the news.] A while ago *[Mr. X]* died. *[Explain who he was and how you knew of him.]* His friends and relatives had a funeral for him. They met together and talked about what they liked best about him. They cried because they are going to miss him.

When someone dies, the people who knew him are sad. But the person who dies is not sad. The person who dies is not lonely. A person who is dead doesn't know anything or do anything or feel anything.

When people are born, God gives them life.

[Light a candle and watch it for a little while.] When people die, they are not alive anymore. *[Blow out the candle.]* But Jesus does not forget about them.

When Jesus comes again, He will give people back their lives. *[Light the candle again.]* Jesus will call the people who chose to believe in Him. They will be alive again. Jesus will take them to heaven.

The people who loved *[Mr. X]* are sad because they will miss him for now. But they are happy because they know they will see him again when Jesus comes.

Dear God, thank You for giving me life. Amen.

Theme: Death and Resurrection

#164

When Jesus Comes

Materials: *a big piece of paper, crayons or markers*

"He will come with great power and glory." Matthew 24:30.

T he disciples wanted to know what it would be like when Jesus came back. So Jesus told them a little about it.

Jesus says that when He comes back, everyone in the world will know it. Everyone will see Him—His coming will be big and bright. Everyone will hear Him—His coming will be loud.

Jesus says that He will come on clouds in the sky. Everyone can see the sky. When you look up, you can see the same clouds that someone on the other side of town can see. When Jesus comes, everyone will be able to look up and see Him.

Jesus says that He will come with great power and glory. When He came to earth the first time, as a baby, He did not come with great power. When He died on the cross for our sins, there was no great glory. But when He comes the second time, He will come like a King—strong and mighty, bright and beautiful.

Jesus says that when He comes, He will blow a loud trumpet and send His angels all around the earth. Everyone will hear. Everyone will see.

Can you imagine what it will look like when Jesus comes again? Let's draw a big picture of what it might be.

Dear Jesus, I can hardly wait to see You coming. Amen.

#165

Theme: Christ's Second Coming

We Will Be With Jesus

Materials: *two paper clips; a strip of paper approximately 11" x 2"*

"We will be taken up in the clouds to meet the Lord in the air."
1 Thessalonians 4:17.

F old paper strip into thirds. Don't actually crease it; just "curve" it. Bring one end of the paper strip to the middle and fasten it in place with a paper clip. *Bring the other end around the back side. Fasten the back section to the middle section with another paper clip on the same side of the strip.]*

When Jesus comes, the believers who have died will rise up to meet Jesus. Then the believers who are still alive will go up to meet Jesus in the clouds.

In that moment everything will be changed. As quick as a wink, we will all be changed. Nothing will ever be the same. The old world will be over. Our new life will begin.

Look at this. *[Grasp the two ends and briskly pull them in opposite directions. The two paper clips will shoot in the air and hitch themselves together.]*

Look, the paper clips are together. It all happened in an instant, as quick as a wink. The paper clips were apart. Now they are together.

The Bible says, "We will be taken up in the clouds to meet the Lord in the air. And we will be with the Lord forever" (1 Thessalonians 4:17).

We will be with Jesus. We will be together.

Dear Jesus, I want to be together with You. Amen.

Theme: Christ's Second Coming

#166

Hold Your Heads High

Materials: *two dolls. Child can use dolls to act out going to the dentist and reacting to the Second Coming*

"Don't fear. Look up and hold your heads high." Luke 21:28.

These dolls get to go to the dentist. This doll likes to go to the dentist. The dentist counts her teeth and tells her she is taking good care of her teeth. He gives her a sticker and a new toothbrush.

This doll is not happy. She never brushes her teeth, so they're in bad shape. The dentist has to work hard to fix her teeth, and she doesn't like it.

Some people like going to the dentist, and some people don't. It all depends on how they take care of their teeth.

When Jesus comes again, everyone who believed in Him will be happy. This is what they have been waiting for. But not everyone will be happy to see Jesus come. The people who didn't believe God will be afraid. The people who wouldn't follow God's plan will not go to meet Jesus. The Bible says they will try to hide.

Jesus says, "When these things begin to happen, don't fear. Look up and hold your heads high because the time when God will free you is near!" (Luke 21:28).

We won't be afraid. We won't try to hide. We will hold our heads high. We will meet Jesus in the air.

Dear Jesus, I will hold my head high when You come. Amen.

Theme: Christ's Second Coming

Come, Lord Jesus!

Materials: *Bible, paper, markers or crayons, glue, yarn or glitter*

"Amen. Come, Lord Jesus!"
Revelation 22:20.

One of Jesus' disciples was named John. John was with Jesus at the Last Supper. He heard Jesus promise, "I will come back" (John 14:3). John was with Jesus when He rose into heaven. He heard the angels say, "He will come back" (Acts 1:11).

From that day on John hoped and prayed for Jesus to come back. He did his best to tell everyone the good news about Jesus.

When John was very old, God gave him a message. God promised John that Jesus would come back. God showed him what it would be like when Jesus came back, and what heaven would be like.

In the last book of the Bible John tells us about that message. [Turn to the last page of Revelation.] At the end of that book, Jesus says, "Yes, I am coming soon" (point to Revelation 22:20).

And John says, "Amen. Come, Lord Jesus!" (verse 20).

That's what John prayed while he waited. And that's what we can pray until Jesus comes to take us to be with Him.

[Make a poster. In large block letters, write COME, LORD JESUS. Let your child decorate the letters with markers or crayons. Or trace the letters with glue and cover them with yarn or glitter.]

Amen. Come, Lord Jesus!

Theme: Christ's Second Coming

#168

D e v o t i o n

Following the Recipe

Materials: *a recipe and the ingredients for brownies*

"Come and receive the kingdom God has prepared for you since the world was made." Matthew 25:34.

Let's make brownies. Here's the recipe— it's the plan that tells us how to make the brownies. *[Follow the recipe step by step. Demonstrate that you have to measure the ingredients carefully. Explain that you must add the ingredients in the correct order.]* It's fun to make brownies. It's fun to eat brownies. But if we want the brownies to turn out good, we've got to follow the recipe.

God has a recipe for this world. He has been following that plan from the beginning. Do you know what we'll have when the recipe is finished? Heaven! In heaven we will be with God. That's what this recipe is all about.

Jesus is getting heaven ready for us right now. He told His disciples, "I am going there to prepare a place for you. I will take you to be with me so that you may be where I am" (John 14:2, 3).

When the time is right, Jesus will come to get us. He will take us to heaven. Everything will be ready for us. Jesus will welcome us. He will say, "Come and receive the kingdom God has prepared for you since the world was made."

God is preparing it now. He's following the plan. He's getting ready to welcome us to heaven.

Dear Jesus, thank You for preparing heaven for me. Amen.

#169

Theme: Christ's Second Coming

Too Wonderful for Words

Materials: *chocolate*

"No one has imagined what God has prepared for those who love him."
1 Corinthians 2:9.

Here's a piece of chocolate. Take a little bite and taste it carefully. Now tell me what it tastes like. It's hard to describe how something tastes, isn't it? We can say it tastes good, it tastes sweet—and then we get stuck. What else is there to say?

Take another little bite. Can you tell me what it **doesn't** taste like? That's a little easier, isn't it?

God showed some of the Bible writers a little of what heaven will be like, and they had a hard time describing it. It was so wonderful they didn't know what to say.

Paul says that we will wear a crown. John says that we will get white robes. Other than that, the Bible doesn't tell us much about what will be in heaven.

However, the Bible does tell us what **won't** be heaven. God showed John that in heaven "there will be no more death, sadness, crying, or pain. All the old ways are gone" (Revelation 21:4).

The old ways are the ways of sin. In heaven there will be no sin. The old ways will be gone. Once the old ways are gone, God's way will make everything good again.

Heaven will be wonderful. Too wonderful for words.

Dear God, it will be wonderful to see heaven for myself. Amen.

Theme: Heaven

#170

Nothing to Be Afraid Of

Materials: *a piece of paper, pencil or crayons*

"And my people will not be afraid."
Jeremiah 23:4.

L et's make a book that will show some things that won't be in heaven. *[Fold a piece of paper in half to make a book with four pages.]* Let's call our book "Things That Are Not in Heaven." *[Write the title at the top of the first page.]*

This first page will show that no one will be afraid in heaven. *[Write "No Fear" at the bottom.]*

Some people are afraid of loud noises, like thunder. Some people are afraid of fierce animals, like lions. Some people are afraid of things that aren't even real, like monsters.

In heaven nobody will be afraid. No one will have bad dreams. There won't be anything scary in heaven.

What are some things you are afraid of? *[Discuss your child's fears, and give reassurance.]*

On this page we should draw a picture of something we are afraid of. *[Choose something and draw it.]* There is a symbol that means "no." It is a circle with a slash through it. When you put it over a picture, it means that is not allowed. Let's put the "no" symbol over this picture. There won't be anything scary in heaven.

Dear God, thank You that I won't be afraid in heaven. Amen.

#171

Theme: Heaven

No More Fighting

Materials: *the book you started in the last session; pencil or crayons*

"Nations will no longer fight other nations." Isaiah 2:4.

L et's make another page in our book about things that won't be in heaven. This page will show that there won't be any fighting in heaven. *[Write "No Fighting" at the bottom of page 2.]*

Don't you hate it when people yell at each other? It bothers me when people argue and get mad at each other. There won't be any yelling in heaven. People will get along.

Do your feelings ever get hurt? Sometimes people do things that make us feel bad or say things that make us feel embarrassed. That won't happen in heaven. In heaven people will be nice to each other.

Do you know what a bully is? A bully is someone who likes to frighten or hurt people. In heaven you won't have to worry about bullies. No one will be mean. No one will tease.

Sometimes countries have arguments and go to war. They send soldiers to fight with each other; there are bombs and other weapons. Many people die and lose their homes. War is a terrible thing. There will never be a war in heaven.

Let's draw a picture of fighting. *[Choose something to draw.]* Now let's put the "no" symbol over our picture. There won't be any fighting in heaven.

Dear God, thank You that there won't be any fighting in heaven. Amen.

Theme: Heaven

#172

It Won't Hurt

Materials: *the heaven booklet you are working on; pencil or crayons*

"But then I will bring health and heal the people here." Jeremiah 33:6.

Let's make another page in our book about things that won't be in heaven. This page will show that there won't be any pain in heaven. *[Write "No Pain" at the bottom of page 3.]*

I know one thing you don't like at all. Sometimes when we go to the doctor you have to get a shot. You don't like it because it hurts. I don't like it either. We have to get shots because they keep us from getting sick. But when we get to heaven we won't need them anymore. There won't be any shots in heaven.

Sometimes when we get sick we have to take medicine. We are glad for the medicine because it helps us get better. But we don't like to take it—it doesn't taste good, it costs a lot of money, and it's a big pain. In heaven there won't be any medicine. We won't need it.

In heaven no one will get sick. No one will get hurt. We won't ever get tired. We will be healthy and strong.

Let's draw a picture of something that hurts. *[Choose something to draw.]* Now let's put the "no" symbol over our picture. There won't be any pain in heaven.

Dear God, thank You that there won't be any hurting in heaven. Amen.

#173

Theme: Heaven

No More Goodbyes

Materials: *the booklet you have been making; pencil or crayons*

"Jesus died for us so that we can live together with him." 1 Thessalonians 5:10.

L et's make the last page in our book about heaven. This page will show that no one will be lonely in heaven. *[Write "No Loneliness" at the bottom of the fourth page.]*

I'm thinking of a very sad word. I will give you a hint. Sometimes we do this when we say it. *[Wave a sad goodbye.]* Here on earth we have to keep saying goodbye. Sometimes our friends move away, and we have to say goodbye. Sometimes the people we love die, and we have to say goodbye.

One of the best things about heaven is that we will be with the people we love. Always. No one will move away. No one will die. We won't need to say goodbye anymore.

And the very best thing about heaven is that we will be with God. We won't be separated from God by sin—because there won't be any sin. Sin won't be there to push us away from God. Sin won't be able to push us away from each other. We will all be together, forever.

Let's draw a picture of loneliness. *[Choose something to draw.]* Now let's put the "no" symbol over our picture. There won't be any loneliness in heaven.

Dear God, thank You that we will all be together in heaven. Amen.

Theme: Heaven
LLFJ-25

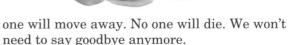

#174

Everything New

Materials: *cardboard, glue, scissors; odds and ends such as fabric, yarn, wrapping paper, greeting cards, pasta, seeds, and leaves*

"Look! I am making everything new!" Revelation 21:5.

Make an art project using odds and ends. Arrange them into an interesting picture and glue them onto cardboard.]

This is a nice picture. It was a lot of fun to make, too. It's amazing that you can take scraps and turn them into something new.

When Jesus' disciple John was very old, God gave him a message about heaven. In the last book of the Bible, John tells us about that message.

John says Jesus is coming back for two reasons. First of all, God wants to be with us. John writes: "God himself will be with them and will be their God" (Revelation 21:3). This is what God has wanted from the beginning. This is

what we are hoping and waiting for.

There is another reason Jesus is coming back. John says He saw God sitting on His throne and God told him, "Look! I am making everything new!"

Our tired old world will be made new. The air and water will be pure and clean. The trees and flowers will be healthy and strong. The animals will be free and unafraid. Our world will be at peace, like it was in the beginning.

God will make everything new.

Dear Jesus, it will be wonderful when You make everything new. Amen.

#175

Theme: The New Earth

Starting Over

Materials: *clear glass, water, red food coloring*

"Then I saw a new heaven and a new earth. The first heaven and the first earth had disappeared." Revelation 21:1.

A while ago we had a story with a glass of water and this red food coloring. Do you remember? We put one drop of red in the water. *[Demonstrate.]* By the end of the story all of the water was red. The red reminded us of sin. When Adam and Eve sinned, things began to go wrong.

Is there any way to take the red out of this water? No. If I want to have clear water in this glass again, do you know what I have to do? First I have to get rid of the red water, then I rinse out the glass, then I fill it up again with clear water. *[Demonstrate.]*

When God told John about heaven, He showed him that first the old things had to be destroyed. Then everything could be made new. Just like we had to get rid of the red water before we could fill the glass with clear water.

God showed John that we will stay in heaven for 1,000 years. Then everything sinful on earth will be destroyed, and the earth will be created all over again.

We will come back to live on earth—this new earth. We will come home—to our home with God.

Dear Jesus, I am looking forward to our new home. Amen.

Theme: The New Earth

#176

Devotion

The Crown of Life

Materials: *lightweight cardboard, foil, stapler, glitter, stickers, markers*

"If you are faithful, I will give you the crown of life." Revelation 2:10.

God showed John what the new earth would look like. John writes that he saw a holy city coming down out of heaven. This city will be very beautiful—made of gold and precious jewels. It will be very big—big enough for everyone who wants to be there.

John says he did not see a temple in this city. Do you know why? On our earth now, the temple and the church are where we go to meet with God. But in the new earth we won't need a place like that. God will be with us all the time, everywhere.

John says that a river will run through the middle of this city. He calls it the water of life.

Growing on both sides of the river there is a very special tree—the tree of life.

We have waited so long for Jesus to come back. But John's dream of the new earth is a dream that will come true. God gave John this message: "If you are faithful, I will give you the crown of life."

Let's make a crown for you to wear. *[Cut a crown shape out of cardboard. Cover with foil. Staple the ends to fit your child's head. Decorate.]*

Dear Jesus, please help me to be faithful. Amen.

#177

Theme: The New Earth

There'll Be Joy, Joy, Joy

Activity: *Talk about things you dislike and like to do.*

"People will not remember the past. They will not think about those things." Isaiah 65:17.

D o you know what I don't like to do? I don't like sweeping the floor *[or some other chore]*. It's boring, and the floor always gets dirty again. But we have to sweep the floor—if it stayed dirty we might get sick from the germs.

Is there anything you don't like to do? *[Get hair combed, get nails trimmed, etc.]* That's a pain, isn't it?

There are so many things on this earth that we have to do: we have to go to bed and pay bills and wear glasses. Sometimes there isn't enough time for doing the things we like.

In the new earth we won't have to worry about these things. We won't need to do all the boring, frustrating things we have to do now. What will we get to do instead? All the things that make us happy—wonderful things we can't even imagine.

Do you know what I love to do? I love to lie in the hammock and read a book *[or some other joy]*. What do you like to do? *[Swim, play with a friend, etc.]* That's wonderful, isn't it?

The things we'll get to do in the new earth will be even more wonderful, more interesting—better than we can imagine.

Dear God, thank You for the wonderful things You have planned. Amen.

Theme: The New Earth

#178

 #179

Together Forever

Materials: *Post-it Notes, crayons, pencil, Bible*

"He will live with them, and they will be his people." Revelation 21:3.

Color five Post-it Notes—red, yellow, green, blue, and purple. On the red note, write Isaiah 35:10. Place it in your Bible by that text, with the red note visible. Do the same with yellow/Revelation 21:3; green/Leviticus 26:12; blue/Jeremiah 31:33; and purple/John 14:3.] The Bible says that in the new earth we will be happy forever and ever. Can you find the red paper that is sticking out of my Bible? [Child finds **red** paper, opens Bible to marked spot; you read Isaiah 35:10.] Do you know why we will be so happy? Do you know the very best thing about the new earth? The Bible tells us. Find the **yellow** paper. [Read Revelation 21:3] We will be with God. That has been God's plan all along.

When God rescued the Israelites from slavery in Egypt, He made a promise. Find the **green** paper. [Read Leviticus 26:12.] When Jeremiah the prophet told the people to follow God, he told them God's promise. Find the **blue** paper. [Read Jeremiah 31:33.] Before Jesus died, He made a promise. Find the **purple** paper. [Read John 14:3.]

God promises that He will be with us. God's plan has always been that we will be together. And someday we will be. Forever and ever.

Dear God, thank You for Your plan for us to be together. Amen.

Theme: The New Earth

God's Plan in Time

Materials: *a clock with a second hand, a calendar, paper and pencil*

"His goal was to carry out his plan when the right time came." Ephesians 1:10.

L ook at this clock. This short stick shows the hour, the long one shows the minute, and this skinny one shows us how fast the seconds go by. Tick-tock, tick-tock. Time is always moving forward.

There are other ways to see time. This calendar shows us the year, month, and day. Today is *[show the date on the calendar]*.

Another way to keep track of time is a time line *[draw a line]*. This end *[point to left]* shows what happens first, and this end *[right]* shows what happens last.

We can make a time line of God's plan for our world. What was the first thing that hap-

pened? God created our world. *[Write "Creation" and draw an earth on the left.]*

Then there was sin and God made a plan to save us. What was that plan? Jesus came to earth and died for our sins. *[Write "Saved" and draw a cross in the middle of the time line.]* That has already happened. We have been saved.

The next part of God's plan hasn't happened yet. Do you know what that is? Jesus is coming to take us to heaven. *[Write "Heaven" and draw clouds at the end.]*

Time is moving forward. God's plan is working. Soon Jesus will come to take us home.

Dear God, thank You for Your plan. Amen.

Theme: The Great Controversy

#180

Devotion